Dilan Güneş

THE RESHAPED ECONOMIC RELATIONS BETWEEN RUSSIA AND TURKEY AFTER WESTERN ECONOMIC SANCTIONS

Bibliografische Information der Deutschen Nationalbibliothek: Die Deutsche Nationalbibliothek verzeichnet diese Publikation in der Deutschen Nationalbibliografie; detaillierte bibliografische Daten sind im Internet über http://dnb.dnb.de abrufbar.

www.cartagena-verlag.de

Druck: Books on Demand GmbH, Norderstedt

Printed in Germany

ISBN: 9783981955491

Book Title: The Reshaped Economic Relations Between Russia and Turkey After Western Economic Sanctions

Author: Dilan Güneş

Editor/Reductor: Leonardo Pataccini (PhD)

Reviewer: Gökhan Erkal (PhD)

Abstract

Economic sanctions as a foreign policy tool is used by sender countries to change policy or behavior of a target country. The economic sanctions are multilevel phenomena that not only affects both sides of the action but also have implications for third parties, reshaping the political and economic relations of the sender and target countries with the other states. The effects of the economic sanctions imposed by the West on Russia and Turkey have direct implications for the balance of power in the region and globally. Therefore, this paper aims to examine how did economic sanctions (re)shape the economic relations between Russia and Turkey. In doing so, the paper applies explanatory sequential mixed methods. First, logarithmic regression model was conducted by time series data over the period ranging from 1992 to 2018. The paper confirms that economic sanctions imposed on target countries that already have trade relations increase the bilateral trade between them, especially for Turkish case. Subsequently, content analysis was conducted reviewing annual data starting from 1992 but mostly focusing on 2014 - 2018 period. The analysis shows that because the sender countries are important trade partners in the target countries, to counterbalance the effects of economic sanctions target countries choose to diversify their trade. According to the results, Russia diversified towards Asia and Central Asia while Turkey increased its trade with the EU which is mutual ally of the US and Turkey. Excluding the 2015 plane crisis between Russia and Turkey, the Western sanctions imposed on both countries increased the bilateral trade between them. However, these two countries are the first choice of each other when it comes to trade partner diversification.

Keywords: International political economy, economic sanctions, trade diversification, bilateral trade, Russia-Turkey economic relations, explanatory sequential mixed methods

List of Abbreviations

GDP- Gross Domestic Product

FDI- Foreign Direct Investment

EU- European Union

US- The United States of America

OFAC- U.S Department of the Treasury's Office of Foreign Assets

IPE- International Political Economy

UN- United Nations

UK- United Kingdom

UNCTAD- United Nations Commission Trade and Development

UNFCCC- United Nations Framework Convention on Climate Change

NOEM- New Open Economy Macroeconomics

UNCOMTRADE- United Nations International Trade Statistics Database

WITS- World Integrated Trade Solution

TUIK- Türkiye İstatistik Kurumu

HSE- Gary Clyde Hufbauer, Jeffrey Schott and Kimberly Ann Elliott

RCA- Revealed Comparative Advantage

TII- Trade Intensity Index

TCI- trade Complementarity Index

Table of Contents

CHAPTER 1: INTRODUCTION AND LITERATURE REVIEW *1*

1.1 Introduction **1**

1.2 Literature Review **7**

1.2.1. Historical Overview of Economic Sanctions 7

1.2.2. Contemporary Approaches on Economic Sanctions 9

1.2.3. Bilateral Trade and Diversification 14

1.2.4. Economic Sanctions and Bilateral Trade from a Global Perspective 18

CHAPTER 2: THEORETICAL FRAMEWORK *21*

2.1. International Political Economy (IPE) as a Field **21**

2.2. Contemporary Theories of IPE **23**

2.2.1. Nationalism 23

2.2.2. Liberalism 26

2.2.3. Marxism 28

2.3. Economic Sanctions and Bilateral Trade in The Field of IPE **29**

2.4. Economic Sanctions and Bilateral Trade in Terms of Nationalism and Liberalism **30**

CHAPTER 3: METHODOLOGY *33*

3.1. Research Design & Strategy **34**

3.2. Case Selection **36**

3.3. Methods of Data Collection & Data Analysis **38**

3.3.1. Quantitative Methods 38

3.3.2. Qualitative Methods 39

CHAPTER 4: DESCRIPTION OF SANCTIONS AND TRADE RELATIONS *43*

4.1. Western Sanctions Against Russia **43**

4.2. Western Sanctions Against Turkey **45**

4.3. Political Relations Between Russia and Turkey **49**

CHAPTER 5: QUANTITATIVE RESULTS AND ANALYSIS *53*

5.1. Quantitative Results **53**

5.2. Analysis of Quantitative Results **58**

CHAPTER 6: QUALITATIVE RESULTS & ANALYSIS *63*

6.1. Qualitative Results **63**

6.1.1. Revealed Comparative Advantage (RCA) 63

6.1.2. Trade Complementarity Index (TCI) 65

6.1.3. Trade Intensity Index (TII) 66

6.1.4. Evolution of Russian-Turkish Trade Partnership 67

6.2. Qualitative Analysis **71**

6.2.1. Economic Sanctions Process and Outcomes for Each Country 71

6.2.1.a. Process and Outcomes for Russia 71

6.2.1.b. Process and Outcomes for Turkey 75

6.2.1.c. Assessment of Sanctions on Russia and Turkey 78

6.2.2. Bilateral Trade Between Russia and Turkey 79

6.2.3. Trade Diversification of Russia and Turkey 81

CHAPTER 7: SUMMARY & CONCLUSION *89*

List of Sources *93*

Appendix *107*

CHAPTER 1: INTRODUCTION AND LITERATURE REVIEW

1.1 Introduction

A politician and diplomat, Aung San Suu Kyi, once said: "Sanctions and boycotts would be tied to serious political dialogue" (BrainyQuote, 2019) stressing that sanctions are a part of politics. Economic sanctions which have an old history dating back to at least 432 BC, are often used today by sender countries to change their target's policies or political behavior (Hufbauer et al., 2007). After the First World War economic sanctions were considered as a way to replace arm conflicts and after the Second World War sanctions were used to hinder or supplement war (Hufbauer et al., 2007, p.10). Even though in the past the sanctions have been used for military purposes, today, economic sanctions pursue foreign policy goals not simply related to armed conflicts. One of the main intentions behind imposing sanctions is to demonstrate authority in international relations by punishing the target country. Deterrence can also be one of the reasons to impose sanctions on a country. With the sanctions, the sender country aims to deter the target country to follow the international rules. Additionally, sanctions aim to make a change in the behavior or a policy of the target country (Hufbauer et al., 2007). There are three ways in which a target country can choose to respond after being exposed to economic sanctions: one, is to negotiate with the sanction sender countries to ease up the pressure of the economic sanctions; second, to retaliate, and third, to look for alternatives to counterbalance the effects of the sanctions.

In the contemporary world, the use of economic sanctions is a usual resource in foreign policy. Especially economic sanctions imposed on countries like Russia and Iran are often on the agenda. The issue with the sanctions is that it is not only between the sender and the target country but also other countries. In other words, economic sanctions are multilevel phenomena that not only affects both sides of the action (sender and target country) but also have implications for third parties, (re)shaping the political and economic relations of the sender and target countries with the other countries.

In 2014, because of the Ukrainian crisis and the annexation of Crimea, EU governments and the U.S. agreed to impose economic sanctions on Russia. According to the Observatory of Economic Complexity tool, Russia's main export destinations are

China, Netherlands, Germany, Belarus, and the United States. Statistics further show that the EU is the main trading partner of Russia and compose 43% of Russia's trade (Eurostat, 2016). Not only the EU but also imports from the U.S. represent a valuable portion of Russian trade. Therefore, the West aimed to put economic pressure on Russia by imposing economic sanctions. From the intentions listed above, the sanction sending countries punished, deterred and demanded a change in the behavior of Russia. Even though being exposed to very harsh economic sanctions, Russia preferred to retaliate and impose counter-sanctions towards the Western countries. The Western sanctions were containing limitations in the arms trade, dual-use goods export, financial measures, prohibition to satisfy claims, other items and restriction on services (EU Sanction Map, 2019). Additionally, the West decided to implement measures to politically isolate Russia and create economic costs to it by import bans on energy and defense products, an embargo on trade of arms, an export ban on technological equipment related to weaponry (Dong and Li, 2018). Russia imposed counter-measures to the ones that imposed sanctions to Russia, including bans and restrictions on foreign economic activities involving limitations in imports of certain agricultural goods, raw materials and food products. This reciprocal conflict is still continuing, and new sanctions are being imposed on both sides. The fact that this process has not yet been concluded proves that the effects and consequences of the Western sanctions imposed on Russia are an important issue even today.

One of the most debated issues when evaluating sanctions on Russia is whether the sanctions were effective or not. Because Russia is not stepping back from its foreign policy and continue to retaliate, scholars consider sanctions as not effective enough. Russia after 2014 sanctions aimed to minimize the possible impact of the economic pressure by enabling certain economic policies. One of the most important policies was the import substitution where Russia minimized its dependence on the imports and replace the foreign products with the domestic ones. Also, initially Russia kept inflation and unemployment under control which in turn stabilized the economy. Even though Russia took preventive measures to minimize the costs of Western sanctions, still the economic indicators experienced a decline. The reason behind the overall decline is not only the sanctions but also because of the decline in oil prices in 2014.

As stated above, diversification is one of the possible alternative strategies to counterbalance the effects of economic sanctions, especially when they are related to trade. In this context, targeted countries may diversify their trade while negotiating with the sender or retaliating it. In the case of Russia, especially after 2014, it seems that the country has responded to the economic sanctions by turning its face towards the East. On the other hand, Russia with for countries in the region (Armenia, Kazakhstan, Kyrgyzstan, and Belarus) established the Eurasian Economic Union (EAEU) in 2015. On the other hand, Russia's bilateral trade with Asian countries including China and Pakistan increased drastically after 2014. Moreover, in addition to the Asian and Central Asian countries, Turkey has emerged a potential strategic trade partner for Russia.

There is a long-standing commercial partnership between these countries, and this has continued to increase from the 90s to the present day. Although trade relations have never reached a point of completion, it can be said that economic relations have been fluctuating in line with political developments. For example, in 2015 Turkey shot down a Russian jet in the Turkish-Syrian border. After this incident, Russia imposed economic sanctions against Turkey which changed the course of their trade relations towards a negative trend. Because the political tension was high between Russia and Turkey this reflected into the trade as well. Other than this, countries' domestic matters, international matters like the Syrian civil war and external sanctions all have a part in changing economic relations between these nations. Therefore, one of the questions that need an answer is whether the economic sanctions imposed on Russia have an effect on the dynamic between Russian and Turkish economic relations.

In 2018, the US decided to impose sanctions on Turkey because of the arrest and detention of Pastor Andrew Brunson. In the first wave of sanctions, the U.S Department of the Treasury's Office of Foreign Assets (OFAC) targeted Turkey's Minister of Interior Suleyman Soylu and Minister of Justice Abdulhamit Gul for implementing human rights abuse. These sanctions had already affected the Turkish economy negatively but Trump's announcement on doubling the tariffs on steel and aluminum made the situation worse for the economy. Turkish lira started to depreciate dramatically so as the other economic indicators. Turkey is a NATO country that had close relations with the U.S. and known to be aiming to become an EU member for a long time. Therefore, the decision of the US to impose sanctions to one of its allies concerned other countries including EU countries.

The majority of the countries (Germany, France, Italy, Azerbaijan, Russia) criticized the US for their foreign policy. However, Turkey with receiving other countries' support, has made it clear that it would retaliate and impose counter-sanctions against its ally the US. Hence, Turkey has stopped buying electronic products and construction materials and doubled the tax applied to 22 products that are originating in the U.S. (Sputnik, 2018). Like it was in the Russian case, in the Turkish case the question of how these sanctions will affect the relations with Russia remains unanswered.

The relationship between Turkey and Russia changed after the collapse of the Soviet Union, when they started to consider each other more as strategic partners than geopolitical opponents. Despite their differences, Russia and Turkey have significant similarities in political terms and regional aspirations. Both countries have a quite similar political style, characterized by strong leaderships. Likewise, both countries aspire to become great regional and global players, sharing common interests that motivate them to cooperate in international and regional matters. After Turkey was exposed to economic sanctions, it substantially increased the cooperation with Russia. This raised questions about Russia's next step in the relations with Turkey and whether Russia was 'winning Turkey' over the US, since until that moment Turkey presented a balanced politics between two of its big partners. In this context, it is argued that the political and economic effects of the economic sanctions imposed by the United States and the EU on Russia and Turkey have direct implication for the balance of power in the region and globally. Therefore, the main research question of this paper is ***"How did Western economic sanctions reshape the economic relations between Russia and Turkey?"***

The literature on economic sanctions generally investigates the effectiveness or success of the imposed sanctions. One of the most comprehensive studies is Hufbauer et al. in their book called "Economic Sanctions Reconsidered" where they look at 174 cases to examine the success or failure of sanctions. Not only the effectiveness of the sanctions but also its relationship with bilateral trade was studied broadly. Studies investigate the success of the sanctions by looking at the bilateral trade between the sender and the target country or to measure the costs of sanctions to either side. Thus, the majority of the literature presents the issues in the interest of the sending countries while it lacks the target country perspective. A very limited number of studies demonstrate the outcomes and the responses of the target countries after they were exposed to sanctions. Moreover, the studies in the literature generally preferred to conduct large-N or single case studies. The studies that are more focused on economics adopt quantitative methods and the ones that are more focused on political science or IR select qualitative methods.

In order to address the existing gaps in the literature, the present research will conduct and in-depth analysis of these two countries sanctioned by the West. The literature on Russian sanctions was widely studied while the recent sanctions against Turkey were not studied. Therefore, it is considered that combining a well-studied and not studied case together adds a new and original study to the literature. I examine their bilateral trade with each other by analyzing their responses to sanctions. For this, I preferred to use the explanatory sequential mixed method where with quantitative methods I examine the relationship between bilateral trade between Russia and Turkey (dependent variable) and effects of GDP, FDI (independent variables) and sanctions (dummy variable). Following the results of the quantitative part, I conduct qualitative analysis on bilateral trade between Russia and Turkey and bilateral trade with other countries in the context of diversification. Using mixed methods addresses the gap of a single-sided approach to the relations between economic sanctions and bilateral trade. This method enables me to conduct an in-depth analysis. Also, the mixed nature of the methodology suits the best to the international political economy (IPE) theory of this study.

Economic sanctions and its relationship with bilateral trade is a very recent and relevant topic in the field of international political economy (IPE) and international relations. By combining economics, political science and international relations IPE help to understand the complex structure of mutual interaction between economics and politics. Not only global problems but also how foreign policy and economic policies influence each other is an interest of IPE. Two of the IPE theories nationalism and liberalism assist the process of analyzing the economic relations between Russia and Turkey after the Western sanctions.

This thesis assumes that economic sanctions may have an impact on the bilateral trade of targeted countries, leading them to cooperate more economically in order to counterbalance their effects. Therefore, the first hypothesis of this thesis is ***"Economic sanctions that are imposed on two target countries, that already have trade relations, will increase the bilateral trade between them"***. The thesis also argues that the Western economic sanctions have affected Russia and Turkey economically since their trade with the West composes most of their overall trade. Simply, if the sender country has potential leverage over the target country then it is expected that economic sanctions will have an effect on the target country (Hufbauer et al., 2009, p.51). This negative economic effect is inevitable if the sender and the target country have trade relations before. Therefore, while negotiation or retaliating the target countries should think ahead to prevent another possible economic blow. According to these arguments, since, EU's potential leverage is high on Russia and the US's potential leverage is high on Turkey these two countries will need to diversify their trade and economic relations to diminish the impact of the sanctions. Therefore, the second hypothesis of this paper is ***"The bigger the share of trade of the sender in the target, the more target country will need to diversify to alleviate the pressure of economic sanctions"***.

This research addresses economic sanctions which is a very topical subject today and the effect of imposed sanctions on Russia and Turkey is an ongoing process. Therefore, it will be helpful to understand the contemporary economic and political relations between Russia and Turkey, as well as their current relationship with the EU and the US. This paper aims to find out the foreseeable impacts on international economic relations on the region. Therefore, this research will contribute to the literature by exploring economic relations more in-depth with the help of liberalism and nationalism approaches. The rest of the paper will continue with the literature review. In the literature section, I will present the most important studies that demonstrate contemporary approaches to economic sanctions and bilateral trade. The second chapter presents the theoretical framework for the relationship between the two main concepts. The theory chapter will give information on the international political economy field (IPE) and focus mostly on liberalism and nationalism approaches. The third chapter will describe the methodology of explanatory sequential mixed methods that test the hypotheses. The fourth chapter will be a descriptive chapter for sanction. Following chapters combine results and analysis of the variables. The chapter will start with background information on Western sanctions on Russia and Turkey separately, then continue with the quantitative and qualitative analysis. Lastly, I will summarize the main arguments and answer of the research question with the help of hypotheses and conclude the paper with a general evaluation with future suggestions.

1.2 Literature Review

1.2.1. Historical Overview of Economic Sanctions

Even though we see that economic sanctions are studied and are in the news recently, the concept of sanctions dates back to ancient Greece (Hufbauer et al., 2007). Of course, as time goes by the form and meanings and process of economic sanctions changed. Towards the end of the 19th century, we start seeing sanctions more and they are more relevant to today's knowledge than the pre-First World War era. As Hufbauer et al. say "after the First World War was extensive attention given to the notion that economic sanctions might substitute for armed hostilities as a stand-alone policy" (2007, p.10). Economic sanctions were used as a tool to limit the military capabilities of the target countries. Further, in their historical overview, Hufbauer et al. assert that after the Second World War period "other foreign policy motives became increasingly common, but sanctions were still deployed on occasion to force a target country to withdraw its troops from border skirmishes, to abandon plans of territorial acquisition, or to desist from other military adventures" (2007, p.10). After the Second World War, still, the "sanctions are imposed to impair the economic capability of the target country, thereby limiting its potential to wage war or for foreign adventurism. This was an important rationale for the broad-based multilateral controls on strategic trade" (Hufbauer, 2007, p.11). In the modern world, military deterioration is done by restricting a target country's efforts to establish weapons of mass destruction and nuclear capabilities (Hufbauer, 2007, p.12). After the Second World War, sanctions have been employed more regularly, economic sanctions have been imposed to pursue foreign policy goals apart from the ones related to armed conflicts and security. Particularly, the imposed sanctions are pursuing the goal to change a target country's regime either implicitly or explicitly, frequently in the foreign policy disputes framework (Hufbauer, 2007, p.13).

Lektzian and Souva (2003) reported that starting from the 1990s, economic sanctions have many users (such as the United States, Russia, the United Nations, and the European Union, China, Germany, France, Japan, Turkey, etc.) to challenge internal and external problems. The study conducted by Hufbauer et al. demonstrate that the United States has deployed sanctions 109 times (either alone or with its allies), sequentially, the

UN imposed sanctions 20 times, the UK by cooperating with its allies has deployed sanctions 16 times and the EU used it 14 times (2007, p.17).

The relevance of economic sanctions keeps its importance even today because many countries especially the Western countries practice sanctions against target countries. Recent studies show that there is an increase in the number of studies related to sanctions since many countries especially the U.S. and the EU use them as a tool. Economic sanctions persist being a universal foreign policy tool that is used by states to challenge them to make a change in the behavior of the target country (Afesorgbor & Mahadevan, 2016). Sanctions are preferable because it is less violent than wars, less harmful than violating international law (Gottemoeller, 2007). Currently, states do not prefer to wage war in a conflicting situation, rather they prefer to impose sanctions (economic sanctions, smart sanctions, etc.) because the cost of imposing sanctions is less than using armed forces. Sending soldiers to somewhere push up the internal domestic cost, and if there are casualties then the cost becomes even higher with the internal political costs. However, sanctions are a way to punish another country without taking political risks of sending people to fight and possibly to die. It is obvious that sanctions are less chaotic than wars but still, the literature on sanctions indicates that sanctions have a low success rate. Even though the success rate is low, still many countries today impose sanctions on another country. The literature answers this paradox by asserting that just the threat of sanctions and expectation of a possible conflict "is translated into a short-run concern for relative gains and reputation that varies with the expectation of future threats or conflicts in the bilateral relationship between the sender and target" (Drezner, 1999, p.4). Drezner (2003) proposes that the success rate of sanctions would be over 50% if sanction threats were also included in calculations, therefore, from this one can understand the power of just threatening a target country.

Many write on sanctions because it is a relevant topic that concerns different fields including political economy, economics, political science, and international relations. Actively, the US uses sanctions especially economic sanctions as a foreign policy tool to demand a change in the policies of the targeted country. Especially, the recent sanctions imposed on Iran and Russia were in the spotlight of the scholars. Therefore, in the following subsections, I will give literature insight on economic sanctions and bilateral trade.

1.2.2. Contemporary Approaches on Economic Sanctions

The theme of economic sanctions has been taken up in a variety of ways within the fields of economics, political economy and international relations. These include the effectiveness of the sanctions in terms of success and failure, the political and economic cost of sanctions, political indicators of sanctions such as democracy, party politics, economic indicators of sanctions such as bilateral trade, tariffs, import-export control for the both in the sender and target countries. The study by Kaempfer and Lowenberg (2007) showed that "Economic sanctions include trade sanctions, i.e., restrictions on imports from or exports to the target country; investment sanctions, which include restrictions on capital flows to the target or, in some cases, mandatory disinvestment; and more narrowly-targeted, so-called "smart", sanctions, such as freezing the offshore assets of individual members of the target nation's ruling elite, or travel bans on government officials and party cadres. In all cases, economic sanctions are supposed to work by imposing some kind of pain on the target country, and particularly on its ruling regime, which then alters its policies in order to comply with the sender's demands and thereby avoid further sanctions damage" (p.869). Because in the political economy field the economics and politics are interrelated, the literature on economic sanctions deals with its relation to politics. Relatively, Allen (2005) presents the mechanism of effective sanctions as imposing economic costs on society of the target state, and in turn, the public put political pressure on the government to modify its behavior. Researches show that under some circumstances, the threat or possibility of sanctions may be enough to convince the target country to change its actions (Allen, 2005).

Allen (2005) conceptualizes the sanctions as the bargaining situations in international crisis and she presents a model of crisis bargaining. Her first assumption is that two states one being the sender and the other being the target have a dispute over something which can be a territory, resource, material good or more likely a policy executed by the target state and considered as detrimental by the sender state (Allen, 2005). The process of bargaining between the sender and the target begins with the imposition of sanctions and ends with the termination of sanctions. There should be an actual agreement to stop the sanctions, the inability to continue under economic coercion does not end the period. Researches results that sanctions have two types: those that are designed to enforce the target country to make changes in its behavior, and those that are completely punitive (Dashti-Gibson et al., 1997; Allen, 2005). Sender countries impose economic pressure to bring about a change in not only any behavior but also in political behavior (Allen, 2005). The vulnerability of the target state to economic pressure is necessary for sanctions to influence its behavior. Related to that, Hirschman (1945) and Allen (2005) suggest that powerful states try to reduce their vulnerability to economic coercion and expand the trade dependence of others to them.

The ability or willingness of the sender to impose economic costs and the capability of the target to avoid or bear such costs affects the success of sanctions (Dasht-Gibson,1997), and the decision made by sender and the target to continue, authorize them to renew their thoughts on the other's decision (Allen, 2005). For sanctions to be successful, the target government must concede to the demands of the sender. The two of the factors that are chosen by scholars who conducted qualitative and narrative sanction research, these are the degree to which the target relies on the sender for imports and exports (e.g., Hufbauer et al., 1990; Miyagawa, 1992) and the political and economic stability of the target (e.g., Green, 1983; Rowe, 1993). Early studies on sanctions bring out a couple of factors that affect the success or failure of the sanctions. The literature on the cost of economic sanctions suggests that after the sanctions the target country is presumed to result in massive economic damage to pressurize the target country to reshape its policies as expected by the sender country (Kaempfer & Lowenberg, 1988; Hufbauer et al., 2007; Dizaji & van Bergeijk, 2013; Afesorgbor & Mahadevan, 2016).

A central issue in the field of sanctions is the effectiveness and cost of sanctions to the countries. Some empirical studies address the effectiveness of sanctions with regard to success and failure (van Bergeijk, 1989; Pape, 1997; Hufbauer et al., 2007; Bapat and Morgan, 2009) although some suggest that usage of economic sanctions as a tool to put pressure on target country has narrow applicability (Kirshner, 1997; Marinov, 2005). Van Bergeijk (2013) presents that in the short-run success of sanctions is higher. Hufbauer et al. (2007) focus on goals, success, and failure of sanctions. Some other scholars evaluate the adverse side effects of sanctions on GDP, trade, currency, employment and more in the target and sender country (Peksen & Son, 2015; Neuenkirch & Neumeier, 2015; Dizaji & van Bergeijk, 2013; Yang et al., 2009; Kaempfer & Lowenberg, 2007; Caruso, 2003). Additionally, Afesorgbor and Mahadevan (2016) examine the influence of economic sanctions on the redistribution of income in the target countries. Also, they provide information that the imposed sanctions decrease trade between the sender and the target while a threat of sanctions might increase trade between them.

The question of whether economic sanctions are effective as a foreign policy tool has been extensively studied in over the years. According to Dashti-Gibson et al. the success of economic sanctions depends on the cost of sanctions to the target country, the extent of trade linkages between target and sender, the stability of the target country, the time period of sanctions (1997).

Hufbauer et al. in their book examined the economic sanctions that are applied for certain foreign policy purposes: a) Destabilizing foreign governments; b) Disrupting military adventures; c) Impairing the military potential of a hostile state; d) Achieving "major" policy change; or e) Accomplishing "modest" policy changes. In their findings, they tracked that imposing sanctions to economically or politically unstable states has a better possibility of success comparing to countries that are stable and healthy. Additionally, their outcomes prove that economic sanctions against allies are more effective than the ones against adversaries. Also, according to results, if the duration of sanctions is longer then the likelihood of success is lower (Hufbauer et al., 1985; 2007). Some thought that longer sanctions increase the probability of success (e.g., Brady, 1987; Daoudi & Dajani, 1983). But others argued that the longer the sanctions the less successful they become. Extended sanctions are less successful because sending states are not capable of maintaining the necessary international solidarity (Dashti-Gibson, 1997; Martin, 1992; Nincic & Wallensteen, 1983).

Research shows that the goals of the sender country affect the success of the sanctions. If the goal is to destabilize the target country, then the determinant of success is the stability of the target country. For the goals other than destabilization, using financial/economic sanctions is the most effective way to cause damage (Dashti-Gibson, 1997). Among the different types of sanctions, the most common one is economic sanctions and especially import-export restrictions. Dashti-Gibson explains that restricting imports and exports may demolish the local economy of the target country but especially the citizens rather than the elites who make policy decisions (1997). Dashti-Gibson (1997), Kaempfer and Lowenberg (1992) offered a theoretical argument that financial sanctions are more effective since they impair the economy of public, they may also have a more direct and immediate impact on ruling elites by limiting their access to foreign currency.

As also suggested by Kaempfer and Lowenberg (2007), according to Afesorgbor and Mahadevan (2016), sanctions, in general, include actions such as "tariffs, export controls, import restrictions, travel bans, freezing assets, reduction or removal of foreign aid and severing of diplomatic relationships" (p.3). Further, they ask a question more related to the connection of politics and economics: "If a combination of such economic embargoes does not induce a change in the behavior of political leadership of the target state, then could it be that these political leaders are somehow immune to negative effects of the economic embargoes?" (Afesorgbor & Mahadevan, 2016, p.3). Related to that, Marinov (2005) asserts two different costs that a target country is exposed to, one being the economic costs exposed by population and the other being political costs exposed by political leaders.

Other than the economic burden of economic sanctions there are also political costs that follow resisting and maintaining sanctions, and in order to sanctions to continue, both sender and target states must be willing to bear those costs (Allen, 2005). Political costs are generally in the form of foreign policy efficiency of the national leadership and since losing power is not a desirable outcome for leaders (Miller, 1995), both the sender and the target governments want to jeopardize its power over sanctions (Allen, 2005). Allen suggests that regime type has an influence on the decision to concede, while democratic publics have the ability to exact political costs on their leaders, on the contrary, autocratic societies have fewer avenues of influence (2005). According to Lektzian and Souva (2003), authoritarian leaders change their behavior in response to sanctions less frequently than democracies or countries with functioning multiparty systems.

When connecting the sanctions and its influence on the politics of the target country, we should mention a different type of sanctions which is called smart sanctions. The method of smart sanctions aspires to "hurt elite supporters of a sanctioned regime while protecting the vulnerable within the country as a whole" (Gilligan, 2016, p. 259). Smart sanctions target a specific group especially the ruling elite of the target country while, in a way, protect innocent citizens. Also, arms embargoes, limiting financial aid, travel bans and so on, can all be ways of deploying smart sanctions (Eyler, 2007, p.60).

Smart sanctions that target certain individuals or groups emerged in return for the failure of extensive sanctions imposed against Iraq in the 1990s (Gilligan, 2016, p. 259). As explained by Gilligan (2016), the smart sanctions constructed to punish elites who were supporting the sanctioned regime and at the same time guard the vulnerable population from the possible economic and social problems of the sanctions that are imposed (p.259). Therefore, the actual purpose of smart sanctions is to supply an alternative to damaging effects of sanctions on exposed populations.

Eyler (2007), explains how smart sanctions can change governmental decisions as "If a market for sanctions exists, and smart sanctions can center on interest groups, these groups or the target's citizens actually could change the government's decisions concerning statecraft through a political process" (p.61). Smart sanctions work when thorough travel bans, monetary limitations, and asset freezes the supporters of a government who hold power commence to experience the effects of sanctions personally or on their businesses, then they as a response put pressure on the regime for a change (Gilligan, 2016, p.259).

In the case of smart sanctions, Drezner (2011) asserts that "evidence provides moderate support for smart sanctions being more humane but less effective than more comprehensive measures" (p.102). That is to say, smart sanctions are more humane when compared to other types of sanctions because of the mission of preventing collateral damage but on the other hand, they are less successful in completing the mission of sanctions. Related to this, Hufbauer and his colleagues conclude that "smart sanctions work better as a signaling device than as a coercive measure." (2007, p.139). Smart sanctions are humane for only targeting the ruling elite rather than the whole population of the target country, but the elites of the target country may look for ways to make up their losses. The ruling elite of the target country can alleviate the political cost of smart sanctions by increasing taxes, decreasing wages, limiting provided services (Eyler, 2007, p.61). Not only such governmental constraints but also propaganda can be another way of mitigating the political costs on the ruling elite. Rulers of the target start "blaming the sender for the pass-through costs" (Eyler, 2007, p.61).

Even though the literature on economic sanctions is comprehensive, Dashti-Gibson (1997) suggests that there is an absence of systematic empirical studies of the conditions. Further, he suggests that the existing literature is dedicated to either qualitative case studies or purely theoretical, deductive models (1997). In the literature related to international trade and the effect of sanctions, researchers preferred to use the gravity model. Gravity model foresees that other things equal, the trade between the two countries will be positively proportional to the outputs and inversely related to the distance between those countries (Parker, 2000). Because keeping other things equal are not always possible, Hufbauer et al. (1997) embed supplementary variables (such as high per capita GNP, sharing a common border, sharing a common language and/or belonging to the same trading bloc) to control the factors that might increase trade flows beyond size and distance between states. Hufbauer et al. find a correlation between bilateral trade and sanctions during the time of the trade. Unsurprisingly they find that "the target's import and export trade with the sender usually accounts for over 10 percent of the target's total external commerce" since sender states are usually large economics (2007, p.90). According to their results "interruption of even a small portion of that trade could carry an important message to the target country [...]" (2007, p.90). Furthermore, in successful cases of their study, only a small amount of bilateral trade was involved, and many cases were unsuccessful "even when a high proportion of trade could have been at risk" (2007, p.90). They conclude that if the trade linkages are high the result is more associated with success rather than failure (Hufbauer et al., 2007). Trade relations seem to be a persuasive variable in enforcing outcomes in major policy changes. The pieces of evidence of the study of Hufbauer and other colleagues serve as a reminder that "high levels of bilateral trade do not ensure success [...]" (2007, p.91).

1.2.3. Bilateral Trade and Diversification

Bilateral trade has been extensively studied along with sanctions and many of the studies tried to demonstrate the impact of economic sanctions on trade relations, either between the sender and target country or between other countries. Caruso (2003), in his paper, discusses the influence of international economic sanctions on US bilateral trade with target countries (49 countries). To do so he uses the gravity model for the duration between 1960 and 2000. According to the results of this study, Caruso (2003) achieved a conclusion which suggests that sanctions (broad or comprehensive) have a negative effect on bilateral trade but limited sanctions fail to comply with those results. Apart from that, suchlike research was conducted by Yang, Askari, and Teegen (2004). In their paper, they investigate the impact of US economic sanctions on trade between the US and the target countries, as well as with the third countries. They select the gravity model to come up with results and the period of the study is between 1979 and 2001. According to the results, economic sanctions decreased the multilateral trade between the US and the target states while it increased the trade between the target countries and the EU or Japan.

A considerable amount of studies that connect sanctions and trade chose Iran as their main case, which is understandable since Iran has been exposed to many sanctions. In one of the studies, written by Bigdeli et al. (2013), investigates the impact of economic sanctions on bilateral trade between Iran and its partners. Again, the gravity model is used between 1973 and 2007. The results show that economic sanctions have a negative impact on bilateral trade (Ezzati, 2016). Other studies with the case of Iran, Kazerooni et al. (2015) examines the impact of economic sanctions on the trade volume of Iran with its main trade partners while Kahrazeh and Nikpour (2014) investigate the impact on the export volume. Both studies used the gravity model and got the results suggesting that sanctions have a negative impact on the export volume and on the foreign trade of Iran (Ezzati, 2016).

The literature on bilateral trade associates it not only with economic sanctions but also with the concept of diversification. Conflicting, UNCTAD studies (2004 and 2018) indicates that the relationship between diversification and trade is not obvious since developing countries are heterogeneous in terms of trade and specialization. Nevertheless, a considerable number of studies connect diversification with trade, and I will present the literature on those in the following paragraphs.

Brenton, Newfarmer, and Walkenhorst (2007) analyze various forms of diversification including: "(i) expanding the range of markets into which existing products are sold (geographic diversification); (ii) upgrading the quality of existing products, including agricultural exports; and (iii) taking advantage of opportunities to expand exports of services" (p.1). Economic diversification, according to the UN definition, is a "process of shifting an economy away from a single income source toward multiple sources from a growing range of sectors and markets". In the technical paper on the concept of economic diversification in the context of response measures, the UN presents determinants and impacts of economic diversification. Economic reforms such as trade liberalization, income, GDP and GDP per capita and investment (as a share of GDP) have a positive impact on export diversification. Real exchange rate, inflation, terms of trade, foreign direct investment also are some of the determinants of diversification that concentrate on export value. Lastly, the volume of products, trade volume has a positive impact on diversification (UNFCCC, 2016).

The literature on trade and diversification lacks in answering at the empirical level the question of whether trade in developing countries promotes or prevents diversification (Osakwe, Santos-Paulino, & Doganet, 2018). Therefore, Osakwe et al. (2018) in their UNCTAD research paper explore the link between trade, trade liberalization, and export diversification. Their focus is on developing countries and to discover the relationship between those. They used a large N sample (144 developing countries) between the periods of 1970 and 2015. Their analyses signify that the more a country is open to trade, the more diversified exports it will have. Other data results indicate that the drivers of export diversification are trade and trade liberalization. Other than these, different indicators contribute to export diversification which are GDP, human capital, geography, infrastructure, and institutions. Osakwe et al. (2018) further suggest that the absence of diversification might raise vulnerability to unfortunate external shocks, thus may affect macroeconomic stability.

Caselli, Koren, Lisicky, & Tenreyro (2015), in their study, argue that the openness of markets to international trade may decrease the volatility of GDP when there is a problem (shocks or crisis). They further argue that this can be done by lessen disclosure of domestic shocks and letting countries to diversify the sources of supply and demand (Caselli et al., 2015). One of the main questions asked in international economics is whether the openness to international trade has an effect on volatility. Caselli et al. (2015) try to answer whether there is a correlation between international trade and economic volatility and if so how. Caselli et al. (2015) challenge the view that suggests that trade increases volatility by highlighting country diversification which shows that trade decreases volatility.

In theoretical literature, the relation of trade and diversification leans on the considered model or framework. Long-established trade models advocate that trade encourages specialization, parallel with comparative advantage of the country. However contemporary theoretical trade models suggest that trade expedites diversification

(Osakwe et al., 2018). Dessy et al. (2010) by using a general equilibrium framework, establish that in developing countries, trade can improve diversification and transformation.

According to the related literature, diversification has the potential to contribute to growth and development through many channels (Osakwe et al., 2018). Diversification of exports is a significant trade objective, but limited studies disregard its availability in the global economy as an opportunity to drive export growth (Brenton et al., 2007). According to Jones and Olken (2007), economic growth is greatly bound up with the large and steady expansion of international trade. Nevertheless, Berg et al. (2006) deduce that trade liberalization is also crucial in sustaining economic growth. Even though there is no universal evidence, considerable cross-country studies demonstrate that diversification and growth per capita income are positively correlated. The greater the diversification is, there will be a more rapid growth of per capita income (Lederman & Maloney, 2007; Hesse, 2007; Brenton et al., 2007).

The diversification of exports is considered as a positive trade objective in maintaining economic growth (Brenton et al., 2007). Some scholars associate the diversification of exports with reduced oscillations in foreign exchange earnings, rises in GDP and employment, higher value addition and quality improvements of manufactured products (Hausmann et al. 2006; Osakwe, 2007; Elhiraika & Mbate, 2014).

When talking about diversification, services are usually ignored but actually is a major source. It is a fact that as the per capita income increases the share of services in GDP and employment rate increase. In many developing countries tourism, depending on suitable labor and natural resource endowment, has been an instrument for diversification (Brenton et al., 2007). Cattaneo (2007) explores that countries with different development levels and trade integration use tourism as a tool for their export growth as a part of diversification. Also, further that study underlines that the opportunity of using tourism is not equal in every country when exploring the conditions for entering the market. Cattaneo (2007) stresses the opportunity cost of investment in tourism in countries that have limited natural endowments or security and political stability problems.

Many studies have focused on export diversification while barely touch upon trade partner diversification. Önder and Yılmazkuday (2016) investigate the connection between trade partner diversification and growth. They evaluate the position of the subject country in international trade by regarding the trade partners of the country and the trade partners of their trade partners to measure a country's connectivity. Further, their result shows that trade partner diversification has a positive effect on growth and as country access to better export markets more, the partner diversification increases. Studies also connect partner diversification with exchange rate volatility (Hitt et al., 2006; Hoskisson & Hitt, 1990; Meyer, 2006). If a country has only one direct trade partner then the country is dependent on its partner and to economic volatilities (Önder & Yılmazkuday, 2016). Moreover Önder and Yılmazkuday (2016) suggest that "a country's TPD [trade partner diversification] in international trade can be used as a proxy for two important macroeconomic characteristics of this country: first, a country that enjoys a high quantity and/or high quality of trading partners may find it easier to substitute for financial development by hedging, diversifying, and pooling risk arising from exchange rate volatility because exchange rate risk is distributed among its trading partners" (p.244).

1.2.4. Economic Sanctions and Bilateral Trade from a Global Perspective

A sufficient number of studies have been devoted to the impact of economic sanctions on bilateral trade. Mostly, the studies focus on the success and effectiveness of economic sanctions with a perspective of the sender country. While most of the studies focus on the sender country, its goals, its success or failure, rather less attention has been paid to the responses of the target country or the after sanctions period of the target states.

Previous research has concentrated on using macroeconomic models to investigate on sanctions, rather than considering interdisciplinary theories/approaches that may help to examine sanctions. Many papers use the gravity model to measure the trade between two countries based on certain factors such as distance, size, language, culture to find the effects of sanctions on trade. Another model is the New Open Economy Macroeconomics (NOEM) model which is a theoretical framework for policy analysis in an open economy that focuses on exchange rate fluctuations and as a result shows the effects of sanctions on the economy (Eyler; 2007).

So far, investigations have been confined to factors and effects of economic sanctions, leaving the question of the target country's behavior towards diversification as a reaction to sanctions. In their research scholars investigate on sanctions by changing their factors, some look at investment, some exchange rates, some trade and so on, but limited studies connect economic sanctions to diversification.

The literature on sanctions especially economic sanctions focuses more on its impacts on both the sender and target countries or more on the effectiveness and success of the economic sanctions. Some studies especially Eyler (2007) and Kaempfer and Lowenberg (2007) with an international political economy approach emphasize more on the trade relations slightly open the door to diversification concept. Nevertheless, there is a restricted amount of studies about how to alleviate the pressure of economic sanctions and trade diversification as a possible way to do so. According to the options of the decision-making process, the target country has a binary option of settle down the sender or show resistance to sanctions. However, in the international community, there are many different scenarios when responding to sanctions. A third way that a target country can choose to follow after exposed to economic sanctions can be to diversify in search of alternative commercial partners. Trade diversification can be a voluntary activity where the country decides to find new partners while a number of studies analyze diversification as a response to a negative external environment. In this paper, I use trade diversification as a defensive strategy which can be considered as positive since it gives the target country the freedom to choose its next movement. Most studies have not explained whether a target country chooses to diversify its trade relations to ease up the pressure of the economic sanctions that are imposed by a sender country that has a large trade share in the target country.

This study will focus on the diversification concept while alleviating the pressure of economic sanctions. Diversification as a concept requires a detailed examination of trade relations between countries. Therefore, this study meets the deficit in the economic sanctions literature and superimpose over responses to economic sanctions.

CHAPTER 2: THEORETICAL FRAMEWORK

The research question of this paper touches upon a very recent and relevant topic in the field of international political economy (IPE). By combining economics, political science and international relations, IPE helps to understand the complex structure of mutual interaction between economics and politics. Not only global problems but also how foreign policy and economic policies influence each other is an interest of IPE. Therefore, the theories of IPE will assist the process of analyzing the economic relations between Russia and Turkey after the Western sanctions.

The literature on economic sanctions and diversification shows that scholars evaluate their research problems either in the field of international politics or international economics but not in the international political economy. Researchers tested their hypothesis by running a model or by doing case studies. The ones looking at economic sanctions within the field of economics tend to use regression models and the ones looking at economic sanctions within the field of IR or political science use case studies with a public choice model which is a theory where economic tools are used to solve problems of politics. Even though in a way the methodology used by the scholars connects economics and politics, they did not explicitly contribute to International Political Economy literature. Since, this study uses two of the main approaches of IPE, first I will start by introducing the field of IPE, following I will present the theory of liberalism and nationalism in the field of IPE, then I will locate economic sanctions and diversification in the field. Finally, I will show how economic sanctions and diversification can be explained through the chosen theories.

2.1. International Political Economy (IPE) as a Field

According to Veseth (2007), the international political economy is a field of social science that pursue to figure out international problems via an interdisciplinary collection of analytical tools and theoretical perspectives. The increasing trend of the IPE field is a result of disappearing borders between politics and economics. Today's problems require a more multidisciplinary point of view for resolution. Al (2015) defines IPE as a new discipline where the interaction between politics and economics is explained in a theoretical and methodological frame. The discipline of IPE became the unifier between economic and political developments. Altan (2013) presents that IPE is about the positive or negative effects of political and economic variables on international economic conditions.

As Veseth (2007) explains, the IPE field is a study of a set of problems which include "international trade, international finance, North-South relations, multinational corporations, and hegemony" and globalization was added to the other set of problems (p.1-3). As explained in O'Brien and Williams (2013), in a time when classic liberal and nationalist theories were seeking to explain interdependence, International Political Economy scholarship appeared in IR. There are constraints and limits to IPE, because of its narrow agenda. One of them is that IPE focuses on trade and financial issues. Lately, IPE scholars show awareness of social orders and sensitivity to the interrelation between domestic and international structures by including the importance of corporate body and civic groups. Analytically, IPE has expanded its agenda by including gender, the role of transnational issues and transnational actors (O'Brien and Williams, 2013, p.36). IPE has a wide perspective since it includes not only IR's war and security subjects but also, subjects on economics. When doing a research IPE makes judgments on the effect of international economic and political relations on the state's internal politics (Al, 2015, p.154).

Politics and economics cannot be separated where the idea behind the emergence of the international political economy discipline. According to one of the first international political economy studies *International Economics and International Relations: A case of Mutual Neglect,* experts of international relations should consider economic indicators and economists should take political factors into account when analyzing a situation (Strange, 1970). Following the idea of political scientists and economists learning from each other which was presented, Veseth (2007) also suggests that it is impossible to consider significant questions of international economics or international politics without regarding their mutual effects. The politics and economics are so interrelated that the political decisions of a state influence international trade and financial flows and consecutively affect the atmosphere where states make political decisions and entrepreneurs make economic decisions.

The IPE discipline consists of three main theories/approaches; nationalism, liberalism, and Marxism. The nationalist approach highlights the concept of states, the liberal approach stresses on the individual and lastly, the critical-radical Marxist approach brings the class notion to the front. I will give information on the nationalism, liberalism, and Marxism approaches in the upcoming section.

2.2. Contemporary Theories of IPE

Different authors use different names for nationalism and Marxism. The first theory/approach of the international political economy is Nationalism, which is also called economic nationalism and mercantilism in different scientific researches. Also, this approach is called Realism but since realism is defined as a theoretical perspective that places security at the center of national matters, in this study I will use the terms nationalism and mercantilism interchangeably.

2.2.1. Nationalism

The history of nationalism or mercantilism dates back to the 15th century during the emergence of the nation-state (O'Brien and Williams, 2004, p. 14) and also rooted back in the 17th and 18th century with the theories explaining the relationship between state power and economic activity (Oatley, 2004, p. 9). The mercantilist approach had an influence on the politics of Western Europe between the 16th and 18th centuries. With the effects of the First World War and with the Great Depression mercantilism kept its importance in national politics. Mercantilism is a nationalist and protectionist approach that was applied in two versions, one is state-centric (in Spain and Portugal) and the other one is the bourgeoisie centric (in Holland and England) (Al, 2015, p.148). Friedrich List, a representative of nationalist thought advocated that the economy of states is above the economy of individuals (Al, 2015, p. 148). As Oatley (2004) lists, classical nationalists comply with three propositions. Firstly, they argue that there is a close relationship between national power and wealth. When a nation state is wealthy that wealth should accrue power. Secondly, trade is considered as a way of obtaining wealth from abroad. In other words, wealth can be obtained through trade as long as there is a surplus, therefore a positive balance of trade. Lastly, classical nationalists assert that certain types of economic activity such as manufacturing activities are more valuable than other types of economic activity such as agriculture or nonmanufacturing activities.

Modern nationalists follow all the propositions of classical nationalists and claim that national power can be acquired through economic strength. Moreover, they argue that in trade, exports should be encouraged while imports should be limited and furthermore, some commodities are profitable than others (p. 9). While classical nationalism focused on achieving wealth and power through non-equalist foreign trade, economic nationalism focused on internal developments in the economy. By the 1840s, economic nationalism gained serious popularity. Alexander Hamilton suggested that state activity is needed to establish a strong manufacturing and industrial structure in the country. Furthermore, he asserted that a country needs commercial protectionism for new emerging industries. Friedrich List, the 19th-century German political economist, was a stricter proponent of economic nationalism, and in the form of education, technology, and industry, he thought that the state must take action in order to revive productive power. According to List, production power was far more important than wealth itself. The list also thought that the most essential foundation for creating wealth and power was the industry, not agriculture (Altan, 2013, p.31).

Mercantilism is an approach that advocates an external trade policy that protects the local economy with interventionist policies. According to nationalism or mercantilism, the country's wealth and strength depend on the excess foreign trade balance. Therefore, the state aims to restrict imports and encourage exports. Nationalists argue that the main actor is the state, this idea comes from "the emphasis on wealth as a critical component of national power, the insistence on maintaining a positive balance of trade, and the conviction that some types of economic activity are more valuable than others" (Oatley, 2004, p.9). There are two assumptions that shape nationalist thought. The first one is the anarchic inter-state system, because of that, each state should preserve its own interests. The second one is the supremacy of the state in political life (O'Brien and Williams, 2004, p. 15). Since the state is the main instrument that people can accomplish their ambitions, the state is the predominant actor both in the domestic and international fields. From the perspective of "economic policy should be used to build a more powerful state", political power shapes market relations (O'Brien and Williams, 2004, p. 15).

Economic activity is significant to authorize certain decisions related to resource allocation which are made through markets. Oatley (2004) suggests that if the decisions are not well coordinated then the economic structure will be inappropriate. Therefore, desirable products from the perspective of national power might be ignored while products that have a limited contribution to strengthen the nation might grow. Moreover, "the country could develop an unfavorable balance of trade and become dependent upon foreign countries for critical technologies" (Oatley, 2004, p.10). The first method of maintaining power, according to the mercantilists, is to reduce dependence on other countries while trading with other countries. Also, to develop domestic markets and to impose heavy taxes on imports in order to be self - sufficient, but at the same time to encourage exports and facilitate the precious metal trade. Therefore, nationalism advocates governments collecting what they have and reducing reliance on other countries and this is self-sufficiency, "the policy is known as autarky which is the pursuit of total self-reliance" (Haynes et al., 2013, p.331). The focus of the mercantilists executes the ways of enrichment of the state, not the individuals. Enrichment of a country can work unfavorably to another country. According to mercantilism, money means power and wealth, and this wealth is obtained with a surplus that is provided from foreign trade.

Since mercantilists consider international economic relations and also foreign trade as a zero-sum game, where one party loses while the other party wins. However, the conflict of the interests of the states is inevitable (O'Brien and Williams, 2004, p.17). Nationalists see foreign trade as an instrument to achieve the state's main goal of maximizing political power. The mercantilist approach exists for the purpose of achieving national security or power, so trade relationships are seen as temporary arrangements that can be easily broken when conditions necessitate other strategies to secure national interests (Barbieri, 2002). For nationalists, the international arena is a competitive environment rather than a cooperative one. Relatively, they reject the liberal theory of comparative advantage due to human nature. In a competitive environment "that is the international political system 'collective goods' will never be acquired and there will be losers as well as winners" (Haynes et al., 2013, p.330-331).

One of the main limitations of the nationalist theory is that it is biased. As can be deduced from the above information, the nationalist view is created in and for developed countries. The main aim of a nationalist is to industrialize the country but for that, the country needs capital, which in that case mainly suits to developed countries. The mercantilists focus only on the nation states, but they have the struggle to explain transnational corporations or MNCs. Since such non-state corporations (e.g. IMF) do not trade it becomes challenging to fit them into mercantilism. Furthermore, the role of nation-states is limited in today's world. Consequently, it is troubling to update the nationalist IPE theory.

2.2.2. Liberalism

Liberalism is the second traditional approach to IPE. The roots of liberalism date back to 18th and 19th century Britain during the times of the industrial revolution. After World War II, in the early years of the Cold War, the international political economy remained relatively open/outward-oriented and economic productivity and growth have emerged. However, in time, as the states are concerned with protecting themselves in an international environment with increasing interdependence and intense competition, it became difficult to maintain outward oriented/open international trade, money and financial systems. With the Bretton Woods system, the advocates of state intervention are called liberals, while the advocates of classical liberalism are called conservatives (Altan, 2013, p. 36). Liberalism challenged the three main propositions of nationalism that I mentioned above. First of all, liberalism pursued to draw a line between economics and politics by suggesting that the intention of economic activity was to enrich people. Second of all, "liberalism argued that countries do no enrich themselves by running trade surpluses. Instead, countries gain from trade regardless of whether the balance of trade is positive or negative" (Oatley, 2004, p.10). Third of all, liberalism challenged the argument of nationalists who were suggesting that by producing manufacturing goods they can become wealthier rather than producing primary goods. Alternatively, liberalism asserted that exchanging the goods that can be produced at home with a low cost with the goods that are produced somewhere else that might cost much if it was produced at home (Oatley, 2004, p.10). In this manner, liberalism suggests that "governments should make little effort to influence the country's trade balance or to shape the types of goods the country produces" (Oatley, 2004, p.10).

The emphasis on the individual activity, on the advantages of market competition, and on restricting the role of the state to what is required to ensure that markets can operate successfully outlines the theory of liberalism (Ravenhill, 2005, p.20). The famous political economists who are also liberals, Adam Smith and David Ricardo were supporting the idea that government should not interfere in the economy and free trade (O'Brien and Williams, 2004, p. 18). Smith presents the argument that the development of a division of labor within a society generates a natural harmony of interests when the 'invisible hand' of market competition turns self-seeking individual behavior into socially beneficial outcomes. Today the invisible hand is the market forces where trade operations and enterprises can perform without governmental interference (Grieve, 1983). Recalling from the nationalist approach, mercantilists concern about the uncoordinated economy that may lead to anarchy, however, the invisible hand supposes that "society would be better off without government interference because it is this that distorts the natural inclination of people to work together, exchange goods and make money" (Haynes et al., 2017, p. 292). Other than the 'invisible hand', Adam Smith with David Ricardo developed a counterstatement to the nationalist approach which is known as comparative advantage theory. The basic idea suggests that some countries have an advantage over other countries in terms of natural resources or the production of certain goods. In an environment where there is no governmental interference in international trade, states can focus on the products they are good at producing instead of attempt to produce everything. Rather than spending effort on producing a product, countries can import goods that are produced in another country. Especially, the theory of comparative advantage assures that even disadvantaged countries can benefit from specialization by "trade[ing] with countries producing goods cheaper than they [countries] were and so usher in an era of much freer trade" (Haynes et al., 2017, p.293).

In the context of the IPE, liberals claim that as long as freedom is ensured both within the country and between the countries, a perfect harmony of interest will emerge, not a conflict of interests. Further, they argue that free exchange between countries will bring about the best possible situation for the countries of mutual trade, as is the case in the free circulation of goods and services within the borders of the country (Altan, 2013). According to liberals, if trade were free all over the world, all countries would have reached the highest level of benefit and economic justifications leading to wars would have been eliminated. Free trade is one of the fundamentals of liberalism. In that sense, governments should have minimum involvement in the international trade processes. In that way, firms are not suffering from protectionist measures and are not facing restrictions on their exported or imported goods.

In line with free trade, liberalism in IPE and liberalism as political thought realize that taking the protectionist policies of government out of the equation brings political gains. Liberals see foreign trade as a vehicle to achieve the state's main goal, maximization of social welfare. Trade relations induce countries to develop political relations (Çakmak and Ustaoğlu, 2017). Democratic peace theory or liberal peace theory postulates that liberal states (democratic states) which have trade relations enhance economic motivation for peace (Doyle, 1983). Relative to liberal theory, democratic peace theory, posits that democracies never appeal to fight each other and often prefer to resolve all the conflicts by establishing peace (Çakmak and Ustaoğlu, 2017). The fundamental reason why democracies are unwilling to fight is the level of their foreign trade (Oncel & Liapina, 2018). Therefore, the relationship between countries not only depends on the interest but also to the benefit and cost (Al, 2015, p.151).

Challenges to liberalism show that countries that are willing to export in an open (liberal) market, might be hesitant to display their own industry to competition. Because of accelerated capital flows other countries may undertake intervening in the financial markets with the purpose of slowing down the movement of money between states or restricting the conditions for investment. With the expanded agenda of IPE, some might challenge liberalism with gender equity, labor rights, and environmentalism. As O'Brien and Williams (2013) further suggest, the common criticism of liberalism is that it undervalues the importance of strong firms and countries and their ability to falsify and manipulate markets (p.17).

2.2.3. Marxism

Marxism originated in the work of Karl Marx as a critical reaction to liberalism. According to Marx, capitalism has capital and labor as its components, and he argued that the value of a good can be determined by the number of labors worked in the production process. However, the capitalist system does not value the labor wages, rather capitalist owners pay less to workers to increase their profit. This situation, as Marx predicted, might lead to a revolution that "would do away with private property and with the capitalist system that private property supported" (Oatley, 2004, p. 11). The focus of Marxism is on class and the interests of labor instead of the interest of the state (O'Brien and Williams, 2004, p.21). A significant scholar Robert Cox (1986) also claimed that focusing on state and avoiding the role of social forces was a mistake. Further, he explained that "social forces are groups of people who occupy a particular place in the global economy by virtue of their role in the organization of production" (O'Brien and Williams, 2004, p.31). The Marxist theory explains the unstable nature of international economic relations in three tendencies of capitalism. First, a natural tendency for profit. The economic competition might lead capitalists to increase their efficiency which will decrease labors' wages and the capital would be concentrated in a small group of elites. Second, uneven development happens when Marx argued that investment increases the abundance of productive capital and decreases the return to capital. Therefore, the profit diminishes in turn wages decrease even more. Third, capitalism leads to an imbalance between production and consumption, either there will be overproduction because of the capital investments or under consumption because of decreasing wages and therefore limited purchasing power (Oatley, 2004, p.11; O'Brien and Williams, 2004, p.23).

2.3. Economic Sanctions and Bilateral Trade in The Field of IPE

The literature proves that sender states make use of sanctions as a foreign policy tool with the aim of a possible change in the behavior of target states. Instead of declaring war and sending troops to another country, after the two World Wars, countries prefer to impose sanctions on their target country as a way of punishment. Because imposing sanctions is a less costly way to punish a target country and a less chaotic way to demand political change. Sanctions mostly include economic conditions that might destabilize the target state' economy which affects the environment of political decision-making. Countries use economic tools under the name of economic sanctions to achieve political objectives. The only approach that allows this transmission between economics and politics is International Political Economy. The field of IPE brings together the interdisciplinary side of itself with the concept of economic sanctions. Therefore, economic sanctions reveal the mutual relation between state economics and state politics. Economic sanctions serve as an economic tool with political objectives since their aim is to change the political behavior of the target country but doing it with economic coercion.

When economic sanctions are imposed to a target country, their bilateral trade relations with the sender country becomes limited. The target country which is exposed to sanctions searches for a way to alleviate the pressure of economic sanctions that might lead to economic destabilization. If the country does not choose to negotiate or retaliate, then as a third option they might choose to diversify, or the target country can do both. In the case of Russia, they retaliate to the Western sanctions as well as they can try to diversify. Also, in the negotiation part, a country can present its conditions for negotiation and on the other hand have different options such as diversification. If the sender and the target state cannot meet in halfway, then the target country has the alternative option to choose to diversify its economy and build different bilateral trade relations with other countries. However, this diversification can happen inside the domestic economy or can happen in terms of changing commercial partners. Diversification of exports within a country would change the products that are imported and exported which in turn change the trade policies and therefore the economic policies. As is seen, one economic decision can change the political environment and further political decisions. Furthermore, a target country may also be in search for alternative commercial partners to trade with, choosing to diversify in terms of trade partners may alter the political relationship between the target and the sender country, as well as the target country and the new partners. Since the concept of diversification is a part of international trade hence it is a concern of IPE.

2.4. Economic Sanctions and Bilateral Trade in Terms of Nationalism and Liberalism

If we recall the literature and the definition of the economic sanctions, we would see that there is a correlation between the liberal approach and the concept of economic sanctions. Liberalism believes that the current global system is capable of generating a peaceful world order. Rather than having an emphasis on military action, liberalism emphasizes international cooperation. The history of the emergence of economic sanctions displays that with time countries disuse military forces in a conflicting situation, instead, they prefer to operate economic sanctions. Globalized society, from a liberal perspective, uses economic tools like bilateral trade to advance political interests rather than threatening force. Likewise, countries make use of bilateral trade agreements to consolidate political bonds between countries. On the other hand, countries manipulate trade relations while imposing economic sanctions as a threat to the target country. Liberals prefer to use economic and social power to achieve their national goals (such as agreements with the neighboring country to help to secure a border etc.). Correlatively, sender countries use economic sanctions to achieve national goals that are changing the policy of a target country.

On the other hand, nationalism is a non-negligible concept when considering sanctions and responses to them. The interests of a country rank in priority according to the nationalist perspective. This idea leads to a protectionist economy as well as valuing wealth and power above all. Foreign trade for nationalists is crucial because the excess of foreign trade is considered as wealth and therefore the power of the state. According to the nationalist view, a country chooses to export more than they import to keep the foreign balance of trade positive. In that sense, a country will minimize its interdependence to another country, by limiting the imports and try to be self-sufficient. In the case of economic sanctions, if the target country is highly depended on the imports of the sender country, the target country will worse off. Either the country will not be able to manage to be self-sufficient and replace the import goods with domestic ones or this weakness will affect the political decisions of the target country. The trade share of the sender country in the target country may affect the dependence of countries to each other. If the target country is not self-sufficient then it may negotiate with the sender country as a response to the economic burden. In another case, the target country may search for other trade partners to replace the trade relations with the sender country and may diversify its economy.

The decision of diversification is an incentive of nationalist belief. Nationalists, in their three propositions, suggest that a country should control how its resources are allocated, in other words, the government should control which products should be produced in order to be competitive in the market and keep the dependence on others at a minimum. A target country, however, can diversify its trade goods and satisfy the need for the import goods by itself. Also diversifying the commercial partners may increase the target country's competitiveness in the market because it can export to different countries where it has a competitive edge.

The overall theoretical approach of this research will be nationalism and liberalism in the field of IPE. Both of the approaches assist us to understand the concepts of economic sanctions and bilateral trade in a more detailed manner. In the international arena, we witness behaviors that have a nationalistic instinct as well as liberal behaviors. In the case of concepts of this study, there is a tension between nationalism (nation-states, export diversification, and commercial diversification) and liberalism (economic sanctions). Therefore, I articulate both approaches to show in a broad way the tension between the sanction sender Western countries and target countries Russia and Turkey. I believe that I give a better account if I use the two IPE perspectives to answer my research question and test my hypotheses.

CHAPTER 3: METHODOLOGY

In this research, my aim is to answer the question of ***"How did economic sanctions reshape the bilateral trade between Russia and Turkey?"***. Hence, I will be using the case of Russian and Turkish bilateral trade after they exposed to economic sanctions by the West. In 2014 with the annexation of Crimea, the Western countries started to impose sanctions against Russia as a punishment and even today it is a topical issue. In 2015, Russia imposed sanctions against Turkey as a reaction to the plane crash crisis. This political crisis between Russia and Turkey resulted in a derogation in trade relations. Since the paper examines Western sanctions, the reciprocal sanctions between Russia and Turkey will not be covered but slightly will be mentioned. Other from sanctions on Russia, the U.S. imposed sanctions on Turkey after the case of Pastor Brunson. In almost four years of period, the West has imposed serious sanctions on Turkey and Russia which have close political and economic relations. Since this topic remains on the agenda, I was interested in finding how those sanctions shaped the bilateral trade between Russia and Turkey.

Answering this question is important, because, economic sanctions are frequently used, and countries might want to observe the possible changes in their relations with other target countries after being exposed to economic sanctions. After all, Russia and Turkey are known to have close relations with each other and the newly shaped bilateral trade relations after the sanctions by the West can be alluring to investigate. Russia and Turkey, themselves, other target countries that have bilateral trade relations with some other target countries and readers who are absorbed in the correlation between economic sanctions and bilateral trade can be interested in this research. Because my results may help countries to rethink of their bilateral trade relations, it may guide Russia and Turkey to shape future expectations and future steps may inform the interested reader. For the investigation process, I will use a mixed method to have an in-depth analysis of economic relations. Many of the studies in the literature, prefer to analyze economic sanctions by using large-N studies and they either use qualitative or quantitative methods. In this study, I will follow a different path and use only two cases and I will analyze them by using both qualitative and quantitative methods. To conduct an in-depth relationship analysis, I preferred to use only two cases and mixed methods.

3.1. Research Design & Strategy

For this research, my design will be a mixed methods design that involves a combination of both quantitative and qualitative research data. The mixed methods design is quite new, which started to be used in research from the 1980s. In the past, the idea on using mixed methods was based on the thought that "all methods had biases and weaknesses of each form of data and the collection of both quantitative and qualitative data neutralized the weakness of each form of data" (Creswell, 2014, p.43). In the 1990s, the mixed methods became the systematic convergence of qualitative and quantitative data. Mixed methods can have procedures as follows "Ways to integrate the quantitative and qualitative data, such as one database, could be used to check the accuracy of the other database. One database could help explain the other database and one database could explore a different type of questions that the other database. One database could lead to better instruments when instruments are not well-suited for a sample or population. One database could build on other databases and one database could alternate with another database back and forth during a longitudinal study" (Creswell, 2014, p.43).

The reason why I chose to use a mixed method is that combining data might provide a stronger understanding of the research problem that is looking at the effects of economic sanctions on bilateral trade between two target countries (in this research between Russia and Turkey). Economic sanctions and bilateral trade in terms of economics can give us numerical data. However, sanctions as a policy and bilateral relations between states have great potential to provide me with documental data. Looking only at numerical data might lack answering the research question, therefore, I will use qualitative data to fill in the gaps provided with the quantitative data. I am planning to explain "quantitative results with qualitative follow-up data collection and analysis" (Creswell, 2014, p.268). Owing to this, the value of the blending of different methods will be to have a more in-depth and detailed analysis of the relationship between economic sanctions and bilateral trade. Not only that but also, I chose mixed methods "because of its strength of drawing on both qualitative and quantitative research and minimizing the limitations of both approaches" (Creswell, 2014, p.267). A mixed method design is ideal for me since I have access to both qualitative and quantitative data.

Practically, such a method will provide a complex approach to research on sanctions and trade that might appeal to those who will conduct further research.

In this research, I will use explanatory sequential mixed methods. The explanatory sequential mixed method is a method where I will first conduct quantitative research. Depending on my results from the conducted research I will build on them to explain them in detail with the qualitative research. It is explanatory since the results of the quantitative data are further analyzed with qualitative data. Nonetheless, it is sequential because there is a sequence starts with a quantitative part and followed by the qualitative part. Because the field of my study is IPE which has a strong quantitative orientation because of the field of economics, this design suits well to the research hence I will begin with the quantitative part.

The data collection of this study will proceed in two discrete phases with accurate quantitative sampling in the first part and with purposeful sampling in the qualitative part. One of the challenges to this study is to form what quantitative results to investigate on in the qualitative part. The main idea is to build qualitative data according to the results from the quantitative part. The results of the quantitative part may be an outlier case, may present important results relating the variables, may show insignificant results, etc. In this study I will first examine the relationship between economic sanctions and bilateral trade, to see if economic sanctions have an impact on the bilateral relationship between to target countries. According to the result, I will get from my logarithmic regression model I will use content analysis where I will be exploring the patterns presented in the previous phase. The nationalist and liberal theoretical perspectives of the international political economy will help to explore economic sanctions, trade and diversification patterns of bilateral relations between Russia and Turkey. The liberal perspective will support the analyzing process of the text and documents as well as the observed patterns in the statistical data.

Data analysis of both qualitative and quantitative databases will be analyzed independently in this method. The results from the quantitative analysis will plan the qualitative follow-up. The significant piece is that the quantitative results will determine the qualitative methods and the questions that should be answered in the second phase. Since the analysis carried out separately, explanatory sequential mixed methods design is useful and straightforward because one database reckons in the other data.

I will interpret the results in the discussion part of the thesis. The interpretation section will start with reporting the quantitative results, then continue with qualitative results. As Creswell (2014) suggests the design will employ a third form of interpretation where I will explain how qualitative results help to explain the quantitative results. The qualitative data will enable me to provide more depth and insight into the results from the quantitative part. A mixed method study seeks to explain the relationship between economic sanctions and bilateral trade and diversification as a consequence while exploring in detail the relationship between the countries after being exposed to sanctions.

3.2. Case Selection

My journey for choosing this research topic started with my personal interest in Turkish-Russian relations. Having Turkish and Russian background will allow me to have a deeper insight into this topic. Already living in an environment where sanctions were exposed and having continuous relations with Russia, adds extra value to what I am trying to answer in this thesis. Therefore, the main case of this study is the economic relations between Russia and Turkey. While looking at the bilateral trade between Russia and Turkey, I will also investigate the impacts of Western economic sanctions on both of them. Additionally, I will examine their responses to economic sanctions individually. The research topic is relevant for the EU since Russia and Turkey are strategic partners and that at the global level Russia and Turkey are big emerging economies and significant regional players.

As we can recall from the literature review, many studies conducted large-N studies with many cases and some focused on one of two cases where they evaluated cases individually and independent from each other. However, in this study, the cases of Russia and Turkey interact with each other through bilateral trade relations in the context of externally imposed economic sanctions. Therefore, there are several reasons why I chose the cases of Russia and Turkey as the target countries of this research, other than my personal interests. One of the reasons that make both countries eligible for being the cases is the fact that they have been exposed to economic sanctions recently (for Russia since 2014, for Turkey in 2018). Russia, after the annexation of Crimea in 2014 faced with several sanctions that were imposed by the E.U and the U.S. The period sanctions started in 2014 and still is an ongoing process. While Turkey encountered with the implication of economic sanctions imposed by the U.S. because of the case of Pastor Andrew Brunson in 2018.

According to the United Nations COMTRADE database on international trade, Russia exports most of its products to Europe (56%, including Turkey). Also, Russia exports by country show that Russia exported $18.21 Billion value of products to Turkey and $10.73 Billion value to the United States in 2017. In terms of imports, Russia imports most of its products from Europe (47%, including Turkey). Additionally, imports by the country present that Russia imports $12.67 Billion value of products from the United States and $3.44 Billion value from Turkey.

In the case of Turkey, the COMTRADE database indicates that Turkey exports big more than half of its products to Europe (55%, including Russia). Turkey exported $8.66 Billion value of its products to the United States and $2.74 Billion value to Russia in 2017. In terms of imports, Turkey imports more than half of its imports from Europe (53%, including Russia). Also, in terms of countries, Turkey imported $19.51 Billion value of its products from Russia while imported $11.95 Billion value of products from the United States in 2017.

What these numbers indicate is the importance of bilateral trade between Russia and Turkey the West, and with each other. Both Turkey and Russia have strong bilateral trade with the West, therefore, the economic sanctions from the West will have an impact on both individually. Other than having bilateral trade with their sender countries, Russia and Turkey have considerable bilateral trade with each other. Since both of the countries are located in Eurasia, relatively close to each other geographically, have similar regime type, have similar interests in the region and are considered allies; choosing them as the case of my study is unsurprising. Moreover, in the context of the global political economy (the empirical term for international political economy), there is a correlation between economic relations and political relations between those two countries. A political issue can easily affect the trade relations and therefore economic relations between Russia and Turkey. For example; in 2015, there was a plane crash incident that leads to a serious conflict between Russia and Turkey. After one of the Russian planes were shot down by Turkey, Russia immediately restricted the trade with Turkey.

3.3. Methods of Data Collection & Data Analysis

The design of this research is the explanatory sequential mixed method, where first I will use quantitative methods and then follow them up with qualitative analysis. Therefore, the methods for each phase will be different than each other but in terms of what they are trying to answer, they will serve together.

3.3.1. Quantitative Methods

In the first phase, I will use econometrics to understand whether economic sanctions have an impact on bilateral trade between two target countries, Russia and Turkey. For doing so, I will have a logarithmic regression which is in a way a modification of gravity model. The reason why I do not apply the gravity model is because of the distance variable does not add any value to what I am trying to answer. I take out the variable of the distance between countries and add new independent and dummy variables which will assist me to have a clearer examination. Since this will be an econometric model, I need many observations which means that I need to take a data series that starts as early as possible. Therefore, the period I am taking is between 1992 and 2019.

Bilateral trade between Russia and Turkey is the dependent variable of this study and so it will be located on the left-hand side of the equation. The indicators of bilateral trade between countries are exports, imports, and total trade. By using the UN COMTRADE data, I find the data of Turkish export to and imports from Russia as well as Russian exports to and imports from Turkey, from 1992 until 2017. I will add the data for 2018 and 2019 from TUIK data. All the data related to imports and exports are in terms of million dollars.

The logarithmic regression estimates the dependent variable, bilateral trade between Turkey and Russia, as $Trade_{All}$. The dependent variable indicates the total trade between country Turkey and Russia (the total of exports and imports). The bilateral trade data are taken from UN COMTRADE International Trade Statistics Database. My trade data sample spans 27 years from 1992 to 2018.

This model also includes several explanatory variables such as the economic size of Turkey (GDP_{TR}), economic size of Russia (GDP_{RUS}). I obtained the GDP data from the World Bank World Development Indicators. The data are in current US dollars and again the sample time is between 1992-2018. Another variable is the foreign direct investment of Turkey and Russia (FDI_{TR} and FDI_{RUS}). I obtained the FDI data from World Bank World Development Indicators. Western sanction against Turkey $SANC_{TR}$ and sanctions against Russia $SANC_{RUS}$ will be the dummy variables of the equation. I obtained the sanctions data from the HSE (2009) data where Hufbauer et al. identified the sender and the target countries of economic sanctions from 1914 to 2000. Additionally, I used TIES data showing sanctions from 1945 to 2005. I completed the data from 2005 on by myself until 2018. I create two separate sanctions table for Russia and Turkey, and I assume a value of 1 when there is an economic sanction imposed by the West, and if there is no sanction in that year, it gets the value of 0. I assume a value of 1 if the sanctions continue even though they were imposed in previous years.

My empirical logarithmic regression takes the general format as follows:

$$\text{Ln}(\text{Trade}_{All}) = \alpha + \beta 1\ GDP_{TR} + \beta 2\ GDP_{RUS} + \beta 3 \ln FDI_{TR} + \beta 4 \ln FDI_{RUS} + \beta 5\ SANC_{TR} + \beta 6\ SANC_{RUS} + \beta 7 \ln \text{Trade}_{t-1} + \varepsilon_{All}$$

In the quantitative phase with the model, I am trying to find out the impact of Western sanctions on the bilateral trade between Russia and Turkey. As I already stated bilateral trade is the total of exports and imports but to understand the bilateral trade, we should look at trade value and trade volume between these two countries.

3.3.2. Qualitative Methods

As stated before, this study consists of two phases, the first one is quantitative and the other one is qualitative. After conducting my quantitative analysis, with the results, I will obtain I will plan the qualitative analysis. The econometric model will give a general answer to the research question and will test the first hypothesis of this thesis. However, as the nature of explanatory sequential mixed method suggest, to have a deeper investigation on the topic I need qualitative analysis.

For this phase, I will use qualitative content analysis which is widely preferred research technique in social sciences. The reason why I chose content analysis is that this research method is used to analyze texts and documents. Hsieh and Shannon (2005) suggest that "research using qualitative content analysis focuses on the characteristics of language as communication with attention to the content or contextual meaning of the text" (p.1278). Another feature of this method that well-suited to this thesis is that the "text data might be in verbal, print or electronic form an might have been obtained from narrative responses, open-ended survey questions, interviews, focus groups, observations or print media such as articles, books or manuals" (Kondracki & Wellman, 2002; Hsieh & Shannon, 2005, p.1278). Downe-Wamboldt (1992) explains that the goal of this method is to "provide knowledge and understanding of the phenomenon under study" (p.314). There are three types of content analysis in social sciences and in this study specifically, I will use directed content analysis.

Directed content analysis has the goal of validating or extending a theoretical framework or a theory conceptually. In this thesis, I am extending my investigation on the bilateral trade between Russia and Turkey after the Western sanctions. Since this is a part of explanatory sequential mixed methods, the qualitative part will follow the general theory that I will discover after applying the econometric model. Hsieh and Shannon (2005) assert that "existing theory and research can help focus the research question. It can provide predictions about the variables of interest or about the relationship among variables [...]" (p.1281). Therefore, by using directed content analysis I can make predictions of variables such as the future bilateral trade between Turkey and Russia, or their future response to the sanctions. Also, I can examine deeply the relationship between sanctions and bilateral trade with the help of content analysis as a follow up to the econometric model.

My key concepts or as referred in the quantitative part key variables have already been identified. For collecting text data on the economic sanctions, I will check the related media articles, presidential statements to understand what kind of economic sanctions imposed on both Russia and Turkey. Presidential statements and certain media sources offer reliable information. To obtain the official documents of imposed sanctions by the E.U. on Russia, I will request for access to certain documents via European Commission External Action e-EEAS Register portal, as well as the open access documents in the official sites of European Commission such as Service for Foreign Policy Instruments (FPI). For the U.S. side of the official documents, I will use the resource center of the

U.S. Department of the Treasury to get access to sanction programs that are administered by OFAC. Moreover, from the official ministerial websites of both countries, I will collect the documents of signed agreements, projects and cooperation. Such documents will help to present and further deduce bilateral trade relations between Russia and Turkey. These documents are accessible in President of Russia (kremlin.ru), Republic of Turkey Ministry of Trade, Ministry of Foreign Affairs. To identify the effects of economic sanctions on the economy I will collect statistical data on certain economic factors such as import and export flows, the balance of trade, FDI, oil prices, exchange rate. I will put account statistical data mainly from WITS, Invest in Turkey, UNCOMTRADE, Eurostat, Ministry of Finance of Russian Federation and the Republic of Turkey, Russian Federal Treasury, Rosstat, TUIK, and World Bank.

For measuring the dependent variable of this study, bilateral trade, again I will collect text data from the abovementioned sources and find documents such as trade agreements between Turkey and Russia. To examine bilateral trade between Russia and Turkey I will make use of some trade indexes such as Revealed Comparative Advantage (RCA), Trade Intensity Index (TII) and Trade Complementarity Index (TCI). For data of these indexes, I will construct the data from UNCOMTRADE and WITS.

In the literature review and theoretical part, I stated that bilateral trade also includes the concept of diversification both in terms of exports and commercial partners. Therefore, to understand whether the Western sanctions of Turkey and Russia lead them to diversify their economy to alleviate the economic pressure of the economic sanctions there are some certain indicators that I need to investigate on. To understand whether economic sanctions have an effect on the decisions of the target country in terms of searching for an alternative trade partner, I will check the trade agreements, trade policies after the economic sanctions including the values of trade with the third countries. While choosing the third countries I will benefit from the documental information on the trade agreements of each country with others. Therefore, again I will make use of statistical data to see trade pattern between subject countries.

CHAPTER 4: DESCRIPTION OF SANCTIONS AND TRADE RELATIONS

4.1. Western Sanctions Against Russia

In 2014 the EU adopted sanctions against Russia due to the violation of sovereignty and territorial integrity of Ukraine including the annexation of Crimea. Moreover, the EU requested an immediate withdrawal of armed forces of Russia and declared that any additional steps taken by the Russian Federation to destabilize Ukraine would have economic and political consequences. The Council of Europe started to take restrictive measures as a reaction to the aggressive actions of Russia in July 2014. After these first flow of restrictive measures, which I will explain in detail, Russia kept increasing its aggression on Ukrainian territory. Consequently, in September, the Council of Europe decided to take further restrictive measures. According to the EU, the current restrictive measures against Russia will expire in 2019.

According to the Estonian Presidency of the Council of the EU project the EU Sanctions Map (2019), the restrictive measures, in other words, sanctions are listed as arms export, arms import, dual-use goods export, financial measures, the prohibition to satisfy claims, other items and restrictions on services. The EU prohibits the export of arms, as well as technical and/or financial assistance related to arms to Russia and it is prohibited to import arms and materials that are related to arms from Russia. The export of all dual-use goods, the technology used for military purposes in Russia is all banned. Also, such exports to any person, entity or body in Russia which are listed in Annex 4 of Regulation No 833/2014 is prohibited. EU further bans any procurement of technical or financial assistance related to the export of the dual-use goods. Financial measures are stated as follows in EU Sanction Map (2019):

> "It shall be prohibited to make or be part of any arrangement to make new loans or credit with a maturity exceeding 30 days to any legal person, entity or body listed in Annex III, V or VI of Council Regulation No 833/2014 or to any legal person, entity or body established outside the EU but owned for more than 50% by an entity listed in Annex III, V or VI of Council Regulation No 833/2014, or to any legal person, entity or body acting on behalf or at the direction of such entity. It shall be prohibited to make or be part of any arrangement to make new

loans or credit with a maturity exceeding 30 days to any legal person, entity or body listed in Annex III, V or VI of Council Regulation No 833/2014 or to any legal person, entity or body established outside the EU but owned for more than 50% by an entity listed in Annex III, V or VI of Council Regulation No 833/2014, or to any legal person, entity or body acting on behalf or at the direction of such an entity."

EU prohibits the satisfy claims in conjunction with any transaction or contract that is influenced by the imposed sanctions. Other than these, additionally the EU listed certain equipment in Annex 2 of Council Regulation 833/2014 and the export of that equipment should be subject to authorization and any financial or technical assistance related to that equipment is also subjected to authorization. Lastly, the EU limits the services that are necessary for the oil exploration and production for Russia (EU Sanction Map, 2019).

Not only the EU but also the US imposed sanctions against Russia due to the Russian aggression in Ukraine. The US sanctions have two main aims; one of them is to demand changes in Russian behavior and the other one is to impose costs to Russia without specifically aiming a policy outcome (Newlin and Mankoff, 2018). Like the EU, the US also made use of restrictive measures as a threat to Russia aiming to show that further steps would have political and economic consequences. Then the U.S. with the E.U implemented tangible measures to politically isolate Russia and creates economic costs to Russia. Some of the economic sanctions that the U.S. imposed on Russia include import bans on energy and defense products, an embargo on export and import of arms, export bans on energy and arms-related equipment and technology, and further financial sanctions (Dong and Li, 2018, p.118).

While the Western world imposes sanctions to change Russia's behavior and put a burden on it, Russia imposes counter sanctions to the EU and to the US. On 24th of June in 2015, Putin signed an Executive Order on extending certain economic measures in order to protect Russia's security and the measures are extended for one year starting on the 6th of August 2015. Under this executive order there are bans and restrictions on foreign economic operations "involving the import to Russia of particular kinds of agricultural produce, raw materials and foodstuffs originating in countries that have decided to impose economic sanctions on Russian legal entities and/or physical individuals, or have joined such decisions" (President of Russia, 2014). Lastly, on June 2017, Putin signed an executive order to extend certain economic measures against the EU in order to protect Russia's national interests from the beginning of 2018 until the end of that year (President of Russia, 2017). This decision was made right after the European Council extended the sanctions against Russia for six months. To summarize, Russian counter-sanctions include import bans from Western counties, travel bans, import bans on textile and consumer products (Dong and Li, 2018, p.118).

4.2. Western Sanctions Against Turkey

In August 2018, the U.S Department of the Treasury's Office of Foreign Assets (OFAC) targeted Turkey's Minister of Interior Suleyman Soylu and Minister of Justice Abdulhamit Gul because they organized the arrest and detention of Pastor Andrew Brunson. An Executive Order was signed targeting Turkish officials for implementing human rights abuse. This sanction is imposed under the Magnitsky Act which was meant to punish Russian officials for the same reason. As OFAC designated, the Turkish officials have limited access to the U.S. financial system and U.S. financial assets are blocked (US Department of the Treasury, 2018).

About the sanctions, treasury secretary Steven Mnuchin said, "Pastor Brunson's unjust detention and continued prosecution by Turkish officials is simply unacceptable, President Trump has made it abundantly clear that the United States expects Turkey to release him immediately." (U.S. Department of the Treasury, 2018). On the same day Minister of Foreign Affairs Mevlut Cavusoglu said "We strongly protest the US Treasury Department's decision to sanction our country. This decision, which targets two of our honorable Ministers, neither complies with state seriousness, not it is explicable within the terms of law and justice. There is no doubt that the decision, which disrespectfully intervenes with our judicial system, stands in contrast to the essence of our relations and will seriously damage the constructive efforts made in order to resolve problems between the two countries. We call upon the US administration to go back on this wrong decision. An equivalent response to this aggressive attitude will be given without delay." (Republic of Turkey Ministry of Foreign Affairs, Press Releases, 2018). Just one day before the Foreign Minister's reaction to the sanctions, President Recep Tayyip Erdogan's spokesman Ibrahim Kalin said that Turkey will retaliate against the sanctions imposed by the U.S. because of the trail of Pastor Brunson (CNN Türk, 2018).

The imposition of sanction and threats from the U.S. side on further economic sanctions against Turkey, and Turkey's threat to retaliate to any kind of sanctions increased the tension between two countries. The aim of the U.S. government is to change the behavior of Turkey by imposing sanctions against it. The sanctions were imposed because the U.S. demanded a change in the decision of Turkey on the trial of Pastor Brunson and demanded the release of the pastor. As I have covered in the first chapters that there are certain ways to react to sanctions; negotiation, retaliation, and diversification while doing one of the others. According to the initial response of the officials, Turkey decided to retaliate to any sanctions.

The first wave of sanctions against the Turkish officials made a tremendous effect on the economy of Turkey. Because of the economic and financial pressure on Turkey, a NATO ally, the Turkish lira depreciated. After this, President Trump announced on Twitter that he "authorized a doubling of Tariffs on Steel and Aluminum with respect to Turkey as their currency, the Turkish Lira, slides rapidly downward against our very strong Dollar! Aluminum will now be 20% and Steel 50%. Our relations with Turkey are not good at this time!" (2018). After these announcements, the Turkish lira depreciated against U.S. Dollar. President Erdogan evaluated this situation as an 'economic war' (Pamuk, 2018).

When as a timeline we look at the restrictive measures that the U.S took against Turkey, we see that things have started in 2017 rather than in 2018. On the 19th of September 2017, the U.S stopped the sale of guns and weapons to Turkish police offices. Then on the 1st of June 2018 the U.S. add tariffs on steel and aluminum that are imported from the EU, Mexico, and Canada. On 19th of July 2018, a draft law that restricts Turkey's borrowing from international financial institutions was submitted to the U.S. Senate. To this respect, the US representatives of the World Bank and the European Bank for Reconstruction and Development have been instructed to oppose future loans to Turkey other than the ones with humanitarian aims. On 1 August 2018, as mentioned before, the sanctions against Turkish ministers were imposed. Then on 10 August, the tariffs on steel and aluminum were doubled. And lastly, on 13 August, the U.S. has suspended the delivery of F-35 fighter jets to Turkey.

As expressed in the previous paragraphs, I stated that Turkish officials openly said that the country would retaliate against the sanctions. Accordingly, on 21 June 2018, Turkey taxed food products from the U.S. The restrictions covered 22 types of products and higher taxes were imposed on alcohol (70%), automobiles (60%) and to tobacco (30%) and on 4 August 2018, Turkey has decided to freeze American banks' assets in Turkey. Also, Turkey imposed sanctions against the U.S. interior and justice ministers. Following this on the 14th of August, Turkey has stopped buying electronic products and construction materials originating in the U.S. Lastly, in the following day, Turkey doubled the tax applied to 22 products that are originating in the U.S. (Sputnik, 2018).

All of these reciprocal conflicts between Turkey and the U.S. caught the attention of the world, and world leaders from Europe, Russia, Azerbaijan, and Iran commented on this situation in support of Turkey. Chancellor Angela Merkel said that "Germany wants an economically prosperous Turkey. That is in our interests too. No one has an interest in an economic destabilization of Turkey, but of course, everything must be done so that, for example, an independent central bank can work and so on." (Hurriyet Daily News, 2018). Additionally, German Economy Minister Peter Altmaier criticized the U.S. sanctions against Turkey by saying "As we saw in the past, consumers are hit by the most in trade wars, which increase products' prices. We need lower tariffs, more open markets and less protectionism worldwide" (Hurriyet Daily News, 2018). Not only Germany but also Italy showed its support for Turkey, Italian Minister Enzo Moavero said that his first thought is "lending its support" and "such a crisis is bad news for all" (Hurriyet Daily News, 2018). Russia, an ally in the region, evaluated these economic sanctions as "counterproductive and destructive". Also, the deputy head of the International Committee of the State Duma, Alexey Chepa, said: "Every day we hear some news that the U.S. either impose sanctions or announces a trade war against those who do not want to act as the U.S. wants,". The member of the International Committee of the Federation Council, Senator Igor Morozov said that "There is no doubt that sanctions destroy trust and because of that, economic, trade and other relations are changing. The U.S. is doing a destructive work leading to self-isolation," (World Bulletin, 2018). Russia's Foreign Minister Lavrov criticize the U.S. sanctions against Turkey in these words: "The situation with threats against NATO member Turkey for Ankara's decision to strengthen its defense capacity by purchasing Russian S-400s is an example, there are many others," and added that the U.S. sanctions as a tool to make countries change their policies (Hurriyet Daily News, 2019). Lastly, Dmitry Peskov, the spokesman of the Russian president, told that "I do not know how this situation [in the Turkish economy] can somehow affect the development of the projects [with Russia]. So far everything is moving along," and "We have very extensive trade and economic relations, companies are intensively operating on a mutual basis, these are the issues, which are traditionally discussed [by the leaders]" (TASS, 2018).

The idea of sanctions emerged with liberal thoughts, ending the arm conflicts and punishing any state that would not obey the rules of international law. Even though the sanctions do not work in every case, still, states use it to punish other states over their illegal behavior. In the case of Russia, the West especially the EU imposed sanctions to punish Russia for annexing Crimea and triggering conflicts in Ukraine. According to the liberal approach to the economic sanctions, the EU using economic sanctions to create harmonious living where all states respect each other and cooperate. The US economic sanctions against Russia can also be considered as liberal in the beginning. But after Trump administration, the course of imposing sanctions has changed. Trump imposed several economic sanctions against a couple of countries including Russia and Turkey. The imposition of economic sanctions even to the allies has made other states suspicious and worried. This concern is due to the possibility of the US making efforts to create dollar advantage and showing its economic hegemony. As we can recall, nationalism is about the power of states and hegemony is a great motivation for countries like the US to impose economic sanctions against others. In the Turkish case, for example, the US interfered with the internal matters of Turkey. Pastor Brunson was under detention and his investigation was ongoing, but the US interfered to Turkish jurisdiction. Therefore, the US acted alone, moved by individual interests; while in the case of Russia it was the Western community acting and based on principles of international scope. Consequently, the American sanctions turned into a trade war with Turkey. Using tariffs and import taxes is a typical nationalist/protectionist measure. Conversely, in the case of Russia, tariffs were not used. In fact, the American behavior with Turkey is aligned with a change in the American foreign trade policy towards mercantilism. Liberalism excludes government interference while nationalism believes that the government should interfere. Therefore, economic sanctions under Trump administration became a tool for nationalist interests rather than a tool to create cooperation and peace by warning/punishing other states for violating international law.

4.3. Political Relations Between Russia and Turkey

The relationship between Turkey and Russia dates back to Soviet times. But after the collapse of the Soviet Union, the image of Russia for Turkey has changed from the geopolitical opponent to more of a strategic partner. Additionally, Özdal et al. (2013) asserts that after Putin became the president and AK party in Turkey came to power, Russia and Turkey increased their multilateral cooperation by expanding commercial relations (p.21) After the collapse Russia lost its global power and regional influence which signaled that it was no more a threat for Turkish national interests and security. Therefore, the bilateral relations between these two countries became more positive (Markedonov & Ulchenko, 2011). There are several documents that based the foundation for the upcoming agreements. One of the oldest documents is the "Friendship and Brotherhood Agreement Between the Turkish Grand National Assembly and the Government of the Russian Federal Socialist Republic" presented in 1921, stressing the significance of friendship and solidarity. There is also "The Treaty on the Principles of Relations Between the Republic of Turkey and the Russian Federation" signed in 1992, "Action Plan Between the Republic of Turkey and the Russian Federation on Cooperation in Eurasia" in 2001 and "Joint Declaration Between the Republic of Turkey and the Russian Federation on Deepening Friendship and Multi-Dimensional Partnership" dated 2004 (Republic of Turkey Ministry of Foreign Affairs, 2009).

In 2009 Turkey and Russia signed seven protocols and intergovernmental agreements. In 2009 joint declaration, as along with the aim to increase trade volume in 2004 Joint Declaration, they "confirm their intention to exert efforts in order to reach common solutions for sustaining and diversifying the bilateral trade in a more balanced way avoiding technical and nontariff barriers". Additionally, both parties stressed the importance of "growth in mutual investments, contracting services, and participation in privatization". Further, in the declaration, they stated that they support land, sea, and railway transportation projects and take steps to liberalize bilateral TIR transportation and improve bilateral trade by building logistics centers in both countries. Also, both parties plan to "support the process of simplifying and speeding up the visa formalities for businessmen as well as facilitating contacts among business circles, chambers of trade and industry, businessmen's associations and unions," (Ministry of Foreign Affairs, 2009). In 2010, Russia and Turkey have established High-Level Cooperation Council and they signed intergovernmental agreements related to trade, agriculture, tourism, construction sector, visa requirements, rail and sea transportation and nuclear power plant at Akkuyu (President of Russia, 2010). In 2011, the conditions of mutual travels of citizens of both countries were declared which is considered as a remarkable achievement in bilateral relations. The good political relations between Russia and Turkey was crowned with Turkey's application for membership of Shanghai Cooperation Organization and its acceptance to become a Dialogue Partner in 2012 (Ministry of Foreign Affairs, 2019).

Nevertheless, Turkey and Russia had opposing views on some certain situations, as well as, conflicts which pitted Turkey and Russia against each other. The Georgian War in 2008 was not a big issue that affected the relations between these two countries, however, Turkey did not let Western and NATO ships to enter the Black Sea and remained neutral. As Torbakov (2008) says Turkey was not satisfied with Russia's actions but it was not frankly confronted Russia. In 2011 the Syrian Civil War has emerged and on the Syrian issue Russia and Turkey have opposing views. Russia supports Bashar al-Assad while Turkey supports the Syrian opposition with the Free Syrian Army. Russia provides arms and financial support to the Syrian government to keep Assad in power. Turkey, however, fights against IS and a branch of terrorist group PKK that are active in Turkey since the 1980s (Pearson and Sanders, 2019).

When talking about Turkish-Russian relations I should mention one of the most serious and recent crises between these two countries, Turkey's downing of a Russian warplane in 2015. On 24 November, Turkey shot down a Russian warplane in the Turkey-Syria border area. Two crew members have lost their lives after this incident. Turkey, in the letter they sent to the UN Security Council, stated that two planes "the nationality of which are unknown have approached Turkish national airspace in Yayladağı/Hatay region. The planes in question have been warned 10 times during a period of 5 minutes via the "Emergency" channel and asked to change their headings south immediately." (SCRIBD, 2015). Following this, the permanent representative Halit Çevik added that one plane left the Turkish airspace while the second one was fired at Turkish airspace, but it crashed on the Syrian side of the border (SCRIBD, 2015). The Russian side claimed that the plane was in Syrian border and remained in Syrian territory throughout the mission. Also, the pilot who survived said that he did not receive any warnings. The unsolved conflict over the downing of the jet has increased the tension between Moscow and Ankara. The press releases and statements from both governments signaled that this incident would have serious consequences. President Putin evaluated this attack as a stab in the back and warned that there would be serious consequences for Russian-Turkish relations.

On November 28, 2015, President Putin signed an Executive Order on special economic measures and on security against Turkey. Russia banned or limited foreign economic operations especially imports of certain goods originating from Turkey; Russia banned or limited certain services rendered in Russia by Turkish organizations; and banned employers, contractors of services not listed by Russia and are citizens of Turkey (President of Russia, 2015). Other than these, Russia suspended visa-free travel between Russia and Turkey, banned charter flights between two countries and strictly controlled Turkish trucking companies (President of Russia, 2015). The official apology of President Erdoğan in 2016 paved the way for betterment of Turkish- Russian relations. In 2016, the relations between the two countries were tested with the murder of Andrey Karlov who was Russia's Ambassador to Turkey. He was murdered at the opening of an exhibition in Ankara. President Erdoğan said "We know that this is a provocation especially aimed at disrupting the normalization process of Turkey-Russia relations. However, both the Russian and Turkish administrations are strong-willed enough not to fall for this provocation." (Presidency of the Republic of Turkey, TCCB, 2016).

After the collapse of the Soviet Union, the way Russia and Turkey consider each other has changed and after the 2000s the relationship of these two counties has been improving. The improvement can be observed by the signed agreements, the presidential visits, and statements that are mentioned above. Of course, throughout the years the relationship between both countries has been tested by the diverse crisis but still Russia and Turkey are powers in the region and are closely interrelated. Igor Torbakov, a political scientist, describes the Russian-Turkish relations as "political dualism," which means that they accommodate both cooperation and rivalry (Markedonov & Ulchenko, 2011).

CHAPTER 5: QUANTITATIVE RESULTS AND ANALYSIS

I will present the results of the study and the discussion of the implications of results as separate sections. In the results section, I will report what the study found in the quantitative and qualitative parts of the analysis. As a reminder from the previous sections, the research question of this study is ***"How did Western economic sanctions reshape the bilateral trade between Russia and Turkey?"*** and the first hypothesis **(H1)** which will be tested in the quantitative part of the analysis is ***"Economic sanctions imposed on two target countries that already have trade relations will increase the bilateral trade between them."***. The second hypothesis **(H2)** which will be tested in the qualitative part as a follow up to the quantitative results is ***"The bigger the share of trade of the sender in the target, the more target country will need to diversify to alleviate the pressure of economic sanctions".***

5.1. Quantitative Results

In the quantitative part, the study tries to test Hypothesis 1 (H1) which is ***"Economic sanctions imposed on two target countries that already have trade relations will increase the bilateral trade between them."***, therefore, I used time-series analysis with a semi-logarithmic regression model by using the ordinary least squares (OLS) method by using Eviews 10 software.

I have a general model where my dependent variable is the total trade between Russia and Turkey ($Trade_{All}$) and the independent variables are GDP of Russia (GDP_{RUS}), GDP of Turkey (GDP_{TR}), FDI of Russia (FDI_{RUS}), FDI of Turkey (FDI_{TR}) and dummy variables are economic sanctions against Russia ($SANC_{RUS}$), economic sanctions against Turkey ($SANC_{TR}$). As seen from Figure 1, clearly there are certain products that are imported or exported more between Russia and Turkey. According to the 2017 values, Turkey exports mostly vegetables, followed by machine and electrics and textiles to Russia, while imports mostly fuel and then metals from Russia. In the case of Russia, it exports fuels and metals to Turkey while imports vegetables, machines, transportation, and textile goods (WITS, 2017).

Figure 1: Turkey Exports to Russia and Imports from Russia All Product Groups (2017)

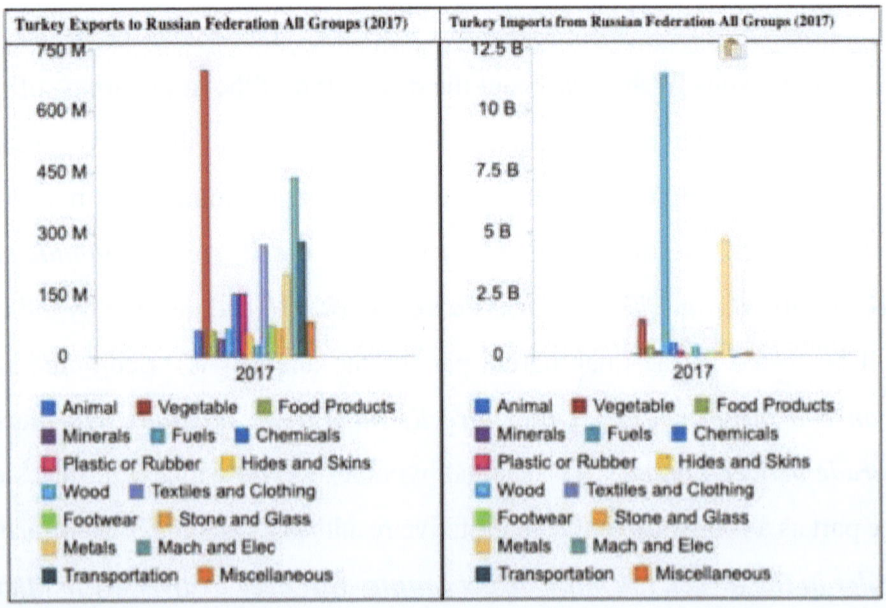

Source: WITS, World Bank (Accessed on 10.04.2019)

Additional to this model I have three more logarithmic regressions to test whether the sanctions have a different impact on different groups of trade products between Russia and Turkey. Fuels, metals, and vegetables are mostly traded products between Russia and Turkey in the period of 1992-2018. These three were determined by the import and export amounts of each product (16 products groups in Harmonized Commodity Coding System (HS)). The data is taken from the World Integrated Trade Solution (WITS) and the Turkish Statistics Institute (TUIK) databases. Then, the total trade of each product was determined, and their average was taken. The top three products which were above the average (fuels, metals, and vegetables) are selected to be included in the model. The general model and following product-based logarithmic regressions can be found in Appendix A.

Before I implement the model, I applied the Augmented Dickey-Fuller (ADF) unit root test to "determine whether a unit root, a feature that can cause issues in statistical inference, is present in an autoregressive model" (Moffatt, 2018). Applying unit root test is necessary since in the time series working with stationary variables is crucial. This unit root test formula is suitable for time series and since economic or financial time series have a complex structure it cannot be simply detected by the autoregressive model but need Dickey-Fuller test. If the Dickey-Fuller unit root test determines that the variables are not stationary and have a unit root, then the first difference will be applied. Nevertheless, as it is shown in the ADF results table, the unit root test showed that the variables are not stationary, therefore, the table also showed the first difference. The first difference of time series displays a series of changes from one period to the following period. The first difference of each variable is denoted as D [ln (variable)].

Table 1. ADF Results

Variable	ADF Statistics	%1 critical value	%5 critical value	%10 critical value	Stationary	H0
Ln (Trade $_{All}$)	-1.113	-4.356	-3.595	-3.234	No	Accept
D [In (Trade $_{All}$)]	-7.481	-4.394	-3.612	-3.243	Yes (%1)	Reject
Ln (FDI_{TR})	-2.767	4.356	-3.595	-3.234	No	Accept
D [In (FDI_{TR})]	-6.601	-4.394	-3.612	-3.243	Yes (%1)	Reject
Ln (FDI_{RUS})	-1.604	-4.356	-3.595	-3.234	No	Accept
D [In (FDI_{RUS})]	-7.504	-4.394	-3.612	-3.243	Yes (%1)	Reject
Ln (GDP_{TR})	-1.426	-4.356	-3.595	-3.234	No	Accept
D [In (GDP_{TR})]	-8.265	-4.394	-3.612	-3.243	Yes (%1)	Reject
Ln (GDP_{RUS})	-1.618	-4.356	-3.595	-3.234	No	Accept
D [In (GDP_{RUS})]	-5.627	-4.394	-3.612	-3.243	Yes (%1)	Reject
Ln (Fuels)	-1.790	-4.356	-3.595	-3.234	No	Accept
D [In (Fuels)]	-5.984	-4.394	-3.612	-3.243	Yes (%1)	Reject
Ln (Metals)	-2.093	-4.356	-3.595	-3.234	No	Accept
D [In (Metals)]	-8.225	-4.394	-3.612	-3.243	Yes (%1)	Reject
Ln (Vegetable)	-2.584	-4.356	-3.595	-3.234	No	Accept
D [In (Vegetable)]	-6.832	-4.394	-3.612	-3.243	Yes (%1)	Reject

Source: Constructed by the author

As can be seen from the ADF results table, all of the variables are not stationary when we first applied the unit root test, at the level. Variables are not stationary because the H_0 is accepted. H_0 suggests that the variable has a unit root. Since they were not stationary, I took the first difference of the variables and all of the variables are stationary at first difference. All of the statistics, as shown in the table, are meaningful at a 1% level. The variables which are stationary indicate that variables do not have a unit root and we reject the null hypothesis. To conduct econometric model that is based on time series regression, it needs stationary variables. This test is compulsory since Granger and

Newbold (1974) provide the information suggesting that regressions with non-stationary variables might result in false results.

After completing the ADF test, I estimate the model by using the least squares method. The results are demonstrated in Table 2. Before diving into the results, first, the focus should be on the explanatory power of the model. To do so we should look at the R-squared index. Also, to check whether there is an autocorrelation problem we should look check the Durbin-Watson value, which should be close to 2. Autocorrelation shows the similarity of time series over time intervals which "can lead to underestimates of the standard error and can cause you to think predictors are significant when they are not" (Field, 2009). Other than these, we should also check the probabilities of the variables in the model.

Table 2. LS estimation results for the models

Variables		Model 1 (All)	Model 2 (Fuels)	Model 3(Metals)	Model 4 (Vegetable)
C	Coefficient	-0.009	0.045	-0.076	0.141
	t-stat	-0.247	0.372	-1.245	1.352
	Prob.	0.808	0.714	0.228	0.192
D [ln (FDI_{TR})]	Coefficient	0.051	0.050	0.040	-0.130
	t-stat	0.961	0.280	0.446	-0.844
	Prob.	0.3484	0.7824	0.6600	0.4088
D [ln (FDI_{RUS})]	Coefficient	-0.031	0.025	0.069	-0.237
	t-stat	-0.686	0.162	0.890	-1.782
	Prob.	0.5006	0.8723	0.3841	0.0906***
D [ln (GDP_{TR})]	Coefficient	0.699	0.365	1.328	0.064
	t-stat	3.765	0.581	4.213	1.581
	Prob.	0.0013*	0.5675	0.005*	0.1302
D [ln (GDP_{RUS})]	Coefficient	0.774	0.360	0.675	0.608
	t-stat	5.846	0.804	3.005	0.120
	Prob.	0.0000*	0.4308	0.0073*	0.9055
$SANC_{TR}$	Coefficient	0.292	0.065	0.234	0.033
	t-stat	3.726	0.247	1.762	0.148
	Prob.	0.0014*	0.8075	0.0941***	0.8835
$SANC_{RUS}$	Coefficient	-0.027	0.126	0.160	-0.208
	t-stat	-0.370	0.509	1.288	-0.981
	Prob.	0.7148	0.6165	0.2131	0.3388
R-squared		0.823	0.080	0.706	0.271

Source: Constructed by the author. Note: *1% significant level, **5% significant level, ***10% significant level

In model 1 where the dependent variable is the total trade between Russia and Turkey, I checked whether the independent variables (GDP of Russia and Turkey, FDI of

Russia and Turkey) and sanctions on Russia and Turkey as dummy variables have an impact on the total trade. As shown in the table the variables GDP_{TR}, GDP_{RUS} and $SANC_{TR}$ have a significant impact on the trade between the two countries. According to the coefficient interpretation, a 1% increase in the GDP of Turkey will increase the trade between Russia and Turkey by 0.699%. The 1% increase in the GDP of Russia will increase the total trade by 0.774%. In terms of sanctions, the sanctions that are imposed on Turkey has a positive impact on the trade between the two countries by 0.292%. By looking at the R-squared value we see that the model has high explanatory power.

In model 2 where the dependent variable is the fuels trade between Russia and Turkey, I checked whether the independent variables (GDP of Russia and Turkey, FDI of Russia and Turkey) and sanctions on Russia and Turkey as dummy variables have an impact on the fuels trade. According to the R-squared value, the model is statistically not significant. Also, GDP and FDI of both countries and the sanctions that are imposed on both are invalid for fuels trade.

In model 3 where the dependent variable is the metals trade between Russia and Turkey, I checked whether the independent variables (GDP of Russia and Turkey, FDI of Russia and Turkey) and sanctions on Russia and Turkey as dummy variables have an impact on the metals trade. As shown in the table the variables GDP_{TR}, GDP_{RUS} and $SANC_{TR}$ have a significant impact on the trade between the two countries. According to the coefficient interpretation, a 1% increase in the GDP of Turkey will increase the trade between Russia and Turkey by 1.328%. The 1% increase in the GDP of Russia will increase the total trade by 0.675%. In terms of sanctions, the sanctions that are imposed on Turkey has a positive impact on the trade between the two countries by 0.234%. By looking at the R-squared value we see that the model has high explanatory power.

In model 4 where the dependent variable is the vegetable trade between Russia and Turkey, I checked whether the independent variables (GDP of Russia and Turkey, FDI of Russia and Turkey) and sanctions on Russia and Turkey as dummy variables have an impact on the vegetable trade. According to the coefficient interpretation, a 10% increase in the FDI of Russia will decrease the trade between Russia and Turkey by -0.237%. Judging by the R-squared value we see that the model has a relatively low explanatory power.

5.2. Analysis of Quantitative Results

By using the explanatory sequential mixed method, I first conducted quantitative methods with the help of logarithmic regression and then as a follow up I applied qualitative methods especially content analysis, to investigate on the question in greater depth. As shown in the results section the general equation of logarithmic regression, it tests whether the GDP, FDI of each country and sanctions imposed on them has an impact on the bilateral trade between Russia and Turkey. According to the results of the first model, the GDP of Turkey, the GDP of Russia and sanctions against Turkey have positive impacts on the bilateral trade between these two countries. Therefore, any increase in one these three variables will result in an increase in overall trade. Before the research started, I was expecting to see a positive impact of some of the variables on total trade especially sanctions. As shown in Table 2, the LS estimation results display no relevance between bilateral trade and sanctions against Russia. This was unexpected since I thought that Western sanctions on both countries would push them closer in terms of economic relations.

To understand the impacts of sanctions on bilateral trade better, I added three more logarithmic regressions. These three regressions test whether sanctions have an impact on traded goods between Russia and Turkey. Since there are many products being traded between two states, I felt the urge to choose some of the products to see the impact of sanctions. Therefore, from the total shares of trade products, I selected fuels, metals, and vegetables as most traded well between Russia and Turkey. Every single regression test one of each and their relationship with the sanctions imposed from outside. The results for fuels display non-explanatory values where I cannot make any interpretation about the relationship with economic sanctions. I was not expecting such results since I thought that sanctions would either increase or decrease the trade of fuels between Russia and Turkey. In the case of regression for metals, two variables seem to have an impact on the metal trade between Russia and Turkey which are the GDP of each country and sanctions against Turkey. Therefore, sanctions against Turkey has a positive impact on the metal trade with Russia. The results for metals closely correlate with the results for total trade. For vegetables, the results suggest that only FDI of Russia has an impact on the trade of vegetables between Russia and Turkey. This result is not very reliable since the explanatory power of the regression is very low (see R-squared values in Table 2).

The studies in the literature review were generally looking at the impact of economic sanctions on the target state and their methods only focused on the trade between the sender and the target country. Depending on this, the results, in general, show that economic sanctions have a negative impact on bilateral trade. Especially the studies dealt with the sanctions against Iran (Bigdeli, 2013; Kazerooni, 2015; Kahrazeh & Nikpour, 2014) presented that sanctions have a negative impact on trade volume, export volume, and bilateral trade. Other studies (Caruso, 2003; Yang et al., 2004), investigating impacts of US economic sanction on trade also showed that economic sanctions decrease bilateral and multilateral trade between the US and target countries. Yang et al. (2004), in their results, demonstrated that the trade relations between the target country and third countries such as Japan and the EU increased after the US economic sanctions. This result paves the way for further analysis on the trade and diversification relation after sanctions, which I will investigate in the qualitative part. As I said, the literature review generally looked at the relationship between the sender and the target, but I am looking at two different target countries and their trade relations after they have exposed to economic sanctions. For that reason, economic sanctions might have a negative impact on bilateral trade between the sender and target country while having a positive impact on bilateral trade between two target countries.

The close economic relations between Russia and Turkey are not secret, therefore, the results may not show a very clear picture to explain the impact of sanctions. What I was expecting is to see that after both countries exposed to sanctions they cooperated more economically. The results of the first regression show that sanctions against Turkey have a positive effect in the trade relations, in other words, after the imposition of economic sanctions to Turkey, its trade with Russia increased. The sanctions against Russia do not have a meaningful effect on trade, not even on the product level. This can be because Turkey is more dependent on trade with Russia than Russia with Turkey. Also, another issue that might affect the results is the plane crisis between Russia and Turkey in 2015, where Russia imposed heavy economic sanctions on Turkey. This issue resulted in a decline in trade between the two states.

The claim of these findings is economic sanctions that are imposed on two target countries will have more bilateral trade with each other. Even though this is the claim still there are a lot of other factors that may or may not affect the results. Lack of data in certain possible independent variables was one of the limitations of this study. For example, the exchange rate is an important variable but since the available data was limited and different in each dataset, I did not include the exchange rate as an independent variable in this study. As I was trying to search for exchange rate data for Turkish Lira to Russian Ruble, I only had access to the TRY/USD or RUB/USD data. I planned to convert the variables myself but, in that case, the numerical errors occurred. Therefore, for the sake of having clear data, I excluded that variable. Another limitation was the sample size. I chose to look at the trade relations between 1992-2018. Since Russia was referred to as USSR before it collapsed in 1991, the data for Russian products and trade started in 1996. Therefore, to overcome this issue I used data from the Turkish side, where I considered Turkish imports from Russia as Russian exports to Turkey from 1992 to 1996. The data is correct because I checked whether the import-export values are complementary or not by simply checking the data from other years. Additionally, since one of my cases in Russia and it was a part of the USSR, I could not expand my sample size towards the past years. Having a larger sample size or in other words, time series might help to ensure a representative distribution of bilateral trade between Russia and Turkey and the impact of sanctions. Another related difficulty was that I chose a period where the last year is very close to the year of research which leads to a lack of available sources. For example, in all datasets generally, I have data until 2017, therefore, I needed to search for additional data just for 2018. Based on this I recommend choosing not a very recent time period for the econometric analysis to improve the data collection process. My dummy variables were economic sanctions against Russia and Turkey, one can diversify the types of sanctions to have a more general picture of how sanctions affect bilateral trade. Most of the studies dealing with this issue preferred to use the gravity model but, in my model, I excluded the distance variable. In further studies, researchers may add distance as a variable to their regression if their cases consist of geographically close countries. Moreover, since other studies generally looked at the bilateral trade between the sender and the target, one can add regressions indication sender-target relations as well.

This paper's first hypothesis (H_1) suggests that ***"Economic sanctions that are imposed on two target countries that already have trade relations will increase the bilateral trade between them."***. I tested this hypothesis with one main and three following logarithmic regressions and according to the results of the main equation, the H1 is partially proven. Based on the positive results of sanctions against Turkey ($SANC_{TR}$) variable, I can say that economic sanctions imposed on Turkey increase the bilateral trade between two states, while I cannot say the same thing for sanctions on Russia. The results for fuel are not explanatory at all and the results for vegetables lacking explanatory power. Therefore, if I only consider overall trade and trade of metals, I can state that both countries' GDP and sanctions against Turkey increased the overall trade and trade of metals. The reasons why Russian sanctions do not have a meaningful impact on the bilateral trade and this study's second hypothesis (H_2) will be discovered with qualitative methods and analysis. There are a lot of factors, as mentioned above the exchange rate, plays an important role in bilateral trade. Therefore, deducing bilateral trade just based on sanctions is complicating.

CHAPTER 6: QUALITATIVE RESULTS & ANALYSIS

6.1. Qualitative Results

In order to analyze the patterns of trade between Russia and Turkey I used revealed comparative advantage of Turkey and Russia, trade complementarity index, and trade intensity index in this section.

6.1.1. Revealed Comparative Advantage (RCA)

Table 3. Turkey RCA for All Products to Russia Between 1996 - 2017

Years/Product	All Products	Capital goods	Consumer goods	Intermediate goods	Raw materials	Fuels	Metals	Textiles and Clothing	Vegetable
1996	1	1,08	1,99	0,87	1,78	0,01	1,25	3,28	2,56
1997	1	1,28	1,78	1,08	1,23	0,01	1,33	4,03	1,62
1998	1	0,45	1,66	1,06	1,49	0,01	1,36	4,57	1,78
1999	1	0,65	2,32	1,05	2,44	0,01	1,28	4,17	2,04
2000	1	0,52	1,47	0,75	2,05	0	0,71	2,61	1,59
2001	1	0,36	1,69	0,62	2,07	0,01	0,84	3,5	2,82
2002	1	0,38	1,76	0,63	1,7	0,01	0,93	6,51	2,68
2003	1	0,47	1,56	0,81	1,66	0,04	0,99	5,61	2,42
2004	1	0,43	1,46	1,08	1,67	0,03	1,1	5,98	2,49
2005	1	0,41	1,36	1,08	1,92	0,07	1,24	6,41	3,42
2006	1	0,58	1,34	0,93	1,95	0,12	0,94	5,63	3,62
2007	1	0,74	0,97	1,19	2,27	0,29	1,23	4,73	3,98
2008	1	0,69	1	1,35	2,19	0,28	0,86	3,84	3,25
2009	1	0,46	1,01	1,1	3,02	0,3	0,88	4,11	5,41
2010	1	0,47	1,12	1,02	3,46	0,29	0,72	4,66	5,15
2011	1	0,65	1,08	1,08	3,34	0,29	0,72	4,65	4,61
2012	1	0,54	1,02	1,29	2,65	0,2	1,02	4,11	4,35
2013	1	0,59	1	1,11	2,74	0,11	0,95	3,81	4,45
2014	1	0,6	0,97	1	2,88	0,23	1,01	3,49	4,48
2015	1	0,54	0,88	0,85	3,53	0,08	0,92	3,35	5,03
2016	1	0,77	0,84	0,85	3,35	0,05	1,12	1,85	3,96
2017	1	0,61	0,94	0,86	3,64	0,25	0,99	2,74	5,02

Source: Data were taken from WITS constructed by the author (Accessed 28.04.2019)

Table 4. Russia RCA for All Products to Turkey Between 1996 - 2017

Years/Products	All Products	Capital goods	Consumer goods	Intermediate goods	Raw materials	Fuels	Metals	Textiles and Clothing	Vegetable
1996	1	0,04	1,66	1,25	1,59	3,41	2,16	0,37	1,97
1997	1	0,04	0,09	1,36	1,57	3,32	3,38	0,3	0,82
1998	1	0,04	0,05	1,38	2,33	3,67	3,56	0,27	1,53
1999	1	0,03	1,33	1,21	2,26	3,64	3,36	0,18	0,69
2000	1	0,02	0,46	1,26	1,46	3,21	2,68	0,16	0,94
2001	1	0,03	0,25	0,68	1,99	3,65	1,81	0,09	0,34
2002	1	0,01	0,77	0,71	1,95	3,93	2,05	0,13	0,52
2003	1	0,01	0,55	0,75	2,04	4,03	2,01	0,15	0,76
2004	1	0,01	0,72	0,86	2,4	4,17	2,34	0,15	0,36
2005	1	0,01	0,81	0,72	2,25	3,75	1,87	0,09	0,26
2006	1	0,01	0,92	0,71	1,91	3,43	1,63	0,06	0,31
2007	1	0,01	0,95	0,64	2,07	3,19	1,35	0,04	0,64
2008	1	0	0,82	0,7	0,68	2,25	1,24	0,02	0,74
2009	1	0	1,05	0,65	0,66	3,1	1,11	0,01	1,3
2010	1	0,01	1,26	0,7	0,57	3,72	1,24	0,01	0,91
2011	1	0,01	0,63	0,75	0,8	1,77	1,44	0,01	1,11
2012	1	0,01	0,72	0,68	0,97	1,84	1,15	0,01	2,48
2013	1	0	0,87	0,71	1,16	2,47	1,36	0,01	2,51
2014	1	0,01	0,82	0,73	1,53	2,28	1,32	0,01	2,93
2015	1	0,01	0,63	0,84	1,86	2,81	1,45	0,01	2,66
2016	1	0,01	0,72	1,04	2,2	3,76	1,89	0,01	3,12
2017	1	0,01	0,85	0,83	1,96	3,69	1,9	0,02	2,55

Source: Data were taken from WITS constructed by the author (Accessed 28.04.2019)

Revealed comparative advantage (RCA) built on Ricardian theory of comparative advantage. RCA postulates "patterns of trade among countries are governed by their relative differences in productivity" (UNCTAD Stat, 2019). Simply, RCA evaluates the export potential of a country. According to the World Bank definition of the index, RCA displays if a country is in action to extend the products in which it has a trade potential. RCA index can also inform us about potential trade partners (WITS World Bank, 2019). If two countries have similar RCA chart, then it is not very likely for two to have high bilateral trade relations. While analyzing the index I will keep in mind that values that are bigger than the break-even point (1) indicates that the country has a revealed comparative advantage in the product. On the contrary, if the value is less than the break-even point (1) indicates that that country has revealed comparative disadvantage in that product.

The RCA tables show Turkey' and Russia's RCA for the selected products to the other one between 1996-2017. I included some certain products in the table rather than every single product group that are traded between Russia and Turkey. The table displays the product groups of capital goods, consumer goods, intermediate goods and raw materials. Additionally, I added the products which are top traded products between Russia and Turkey such as fuels, metals, vegetables and textile and clothing. Three of them (fuels, metals and vegetables) were also used in the logarithmic regression.

6.1.2. Trade Complementarity Index (TCI)

Table 5. Trade Complementarity Index Between Turkey and Russia 2011 - 2017

Year	Trade Complementarity Index
2011	61.23
2012	58.45
2013	62.68
2014	63.01
2015	60.42
2016	59.34
2017	60.25

Source: UNCOMTRADE, structured by the author, (Accessed 23.04.2019)

Trade complementarity index (TCI) measures whether the export pattern of one country matches with its partner's import pattern. The values are between 0 and 100, therefore, if the value is closer to 0 it indicates that the less successful bilateral trade between those countries. On the contrary, the higher the degree of complementarity the better bilateral trade between the countries. This index also provides information for potential regional trade agreements. One of the limitations of this index is that, if there is a high complementarity between two countries which are distant from each other geographically, or their economic sizes are very different from each other, then the results can be misleading (Mikic & Gilbert, 2007).

6.1.3. Trade Intensity Index (TII)

Table 6. Trade Intensity Index between Russia and Turkey 1992 - 2017

Year	Trade Intensity Index
1992	315.08 (3.15)
1993	372.99 (3.72)
1994	541.57 (5.41)
1995	630.44 (6.30)
1996	593.78 (5.94)
1997	706.05 (7.06)
1998	515.69 (5.16)
1999	352.85 (3.53)
2000	343.28 (3.43)
2001	340.97 (3.41)
2002	362.68 (3.62)
2003	286.87 (2.87)
2004	260.88 (2.61)
2005	257.67 (2.58)
2006	275.88 (2.76)
2007	263.65 (2.64)
2008	269.21 (2.69)
2009	236.64 (2.37)
2010	275.79 (2.76)
2011	266.65 (2.67)
2012	249.68 (2.50)
2013	267.62 (2.68)
2014	241.40 (2.41)
2015	225.16 (2.25)
2016	108.96 (1.09)
2017	134.38 (1.34)

Source: Data taken from WITS constructed by the author (Accessed 23.04.2019)

Graph 1. Trade Intensity Index between Russia and Turkey 1992 - 2017

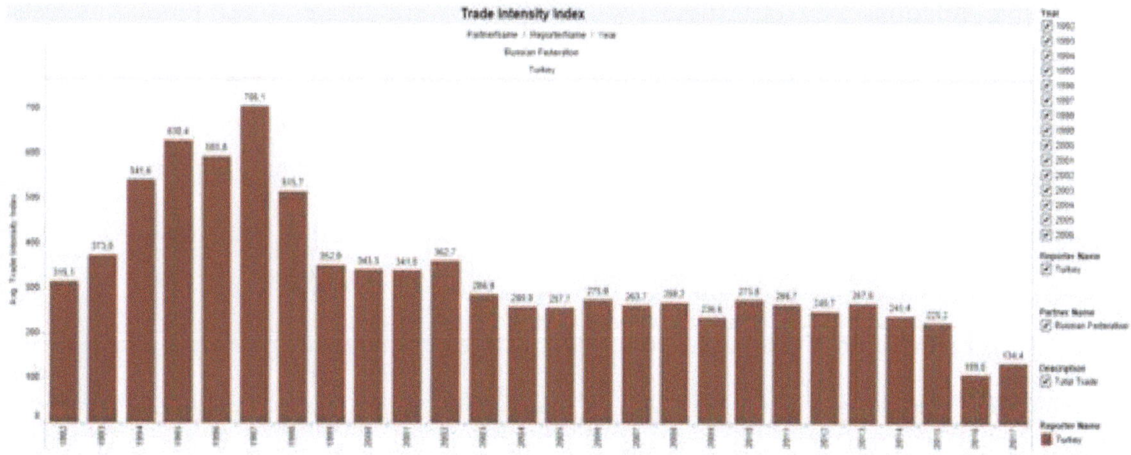

Source: WITS- UNSD Comtrade World Development Indicators (Accessed 23.04.2019)

Trade intensity index (TII) help to determine whether the trade value between the two countries is higher or smaller than the expected trade value according to their significance in world trade. In other words, it measures the trade intensity between countries. TII displays whether the reporter country (Turkey) exports more to its partner country (Russia) than the world. When analyzing the numbers, if the value is bigger than 1, we need to consider that reporter country's trade with its partner country is higher than the world and if it is smaller than 1 then it shows that the trade between two countries is lower than the world on average. TII>1 demonstrates 'intense' trade relations between the two countries. The table and the graph present that the trade between Russia and Turkey has always been higher than their trade with the world on average. After 2014 the TII value decreased from 2.41 to 2.25 in 2015 which can be explained with the sanctions against Russia. From 2015 to 2016 the TII value declined again from 2.25 to 1.09 which is a very big decline for these two countries, and this can be explained with the 2015 plane crisis between Russia and Turkey where they imposed sanctions against each other. After hitting the bottom in 2016, in 2017 the value started to increase from 1.09 to 1.34 in 2017.

6.1.4. Evolution of Russian-Turkish Trade Partnership

As it was the case for the political relation between Russia and Turkey, in terms of economic relations the conflicting visualization of each other give way to a more cooperative bilateral economic relation. The fundamentals of the establishment of better economic relations between these two countries were bilateral economic interests, scientific and technical potential of both countries (Özbay, 2011, p.73). As the trade volume increases between Russia and Turkey they prefer to collaborate more on their common economic interests. Increasing bilateral trade and diversification of trade helped Russia and Turkey to overcome political conflicts, but on the other hand, made economic relations sensitive to political relations or vice versa.

Agreement on Trade and Economic Cooperation signed in 1991, Agreement on Reciprocal promotion and Protection of Agreements signed in 1997 and Agreement on Avoidance of Double Taxation signed in 1997 were some of the agreements that underpin the economic relations between Russia and Turkey. The increase in bilateral trade, mutual investment, touristic visits and cooperation especially in energy sector lead Russia and Turkey to have stronger economic ties.

Turkey managed to build a modernized economic system with a convergence to liberal development. Based on its liberal economy, Turkey made market reforms and had an export-oriented trade. Therefore, with the increasing growth, development and support for exports facilitated the improvement of foreign trade. On the other hand, Russia in the beginning of 1990s, after the collapse of Soviet Union, replaced its socialist economy with profound market reforms. Russia aimed to change socialist economy to a more capitalist economy which was being more market-oriented. Russia's economy has always been very dependent on oil and gas. Turkey and Russia are key trading partners and Russia is a significant investor in Turkey. These two countries are not only cooperating in trade but also cooperate in terms of tourism, investment, science and culture.

Bilateral trade between Russia and Turkey has a positive trend in general for over 20 years. Both countries have economic ties in terms of trade, energy, investment and tourism. Since the collapse of Soviet Union, the bilateral trade between Russia and Turkey has developed rapidly. As shown in the Graph 2, if we avoid the breaking points in 2008, 2014 and 2015, the overall bilateral trade between these two countries has an upward trending graph.

Graph 2. Total Trade (Bilateral Trade) Between Russia and Turkey 1992 - 2018

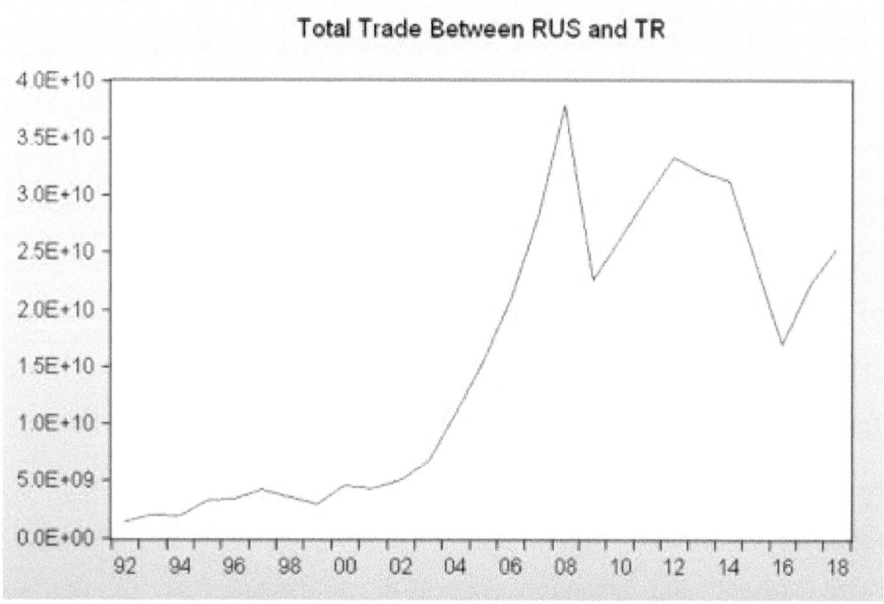

Source: Data taken from UNCOMTRADE. Graph constructed by the author.

The bilateral trade was over $1 million in 1992 and increased to $4 million in 2000. This increasing trend continued until 2008 where the bilateral trade was $37 million. In 2008 a financial crisis hit the world including Russia. Since Russia is one of the main exporters of oil and gas the decline in the price of crude oil in 2008 lead Russian economy to went through a recession. Additionally, in the same year Russian-Georgian War emerged which affected Russian foreign direct investment because of the declining trust of investors. Therefore, the trade between Russia and Turkey decreased accordingly.

In 2014, Western countries, especially the EU, imposed economic sanctions on Russia which lead Russia to enable import substitution economic policy. With protective economic policies, Russia tried to minimize its imports and encouraged domestic production. Also, in 2014 the oil prices again started to decrease which as a result affected Russian economy since it is very dependent on the price of oil. Consequently, the Russian trade with Turkey decreased in 2014.

In 2015, a political crisis occurred between Russia and Turkey which lead Russia to impose heavy economic sanctions against Turkey. The incident where Turkey shot down Russian jet and cause the death of two people, increased the tension between Moscow and Ankara. The economic sanctions mainly affected Turkey's agricultural and tourism sectors. After foreign minister Sergei Lavrov called Russian citizens to not go to Turkey, the tourist numbers and overall tourism receipts prominently declined. According to TÜRSAB (Association of Turkish Travel Agencies) statistics, the tourism receipts were more than $34 million in 2014, this number decreased to $31 million in 2015 and reached its bottom in 2016 with $22 million.

In general terms the bilateral economic ties between Russia and Turkey are strong even though both countries have political issues with each other. Political agendas of both countries have an impact on their economic relations as suggested by the international political economy field. Therefore, external measures like sanctions which affect their economies will lead them to further construct their foreign policy accordingly.

Energy is one of the major common ground for both Russia and Turkey in terms of investment and stronger economic relations. One of the significant agreements signed between Russia and Turkey on cooperation in the field of energy was the Akkuyu Nuclear Power Plant project. The construction and operation started after it was signed in 2010 (Akkuyu NPP, 2019). One of the main steps were taken in 2014 with the TurkStream project which aims to bypass Ukraine and "directly connect the large gas reserves in Russia to the Turkish gas transportation network, creating a reliable source of energy for Turkey, South and Southeast Europe" (TurkStream, 2019). The offshore section of the gas pipeline completed on November 2018.

The investment from Russia to the energy sector increased the overall FDI in Turkey from $12749 million in 2014 to $16800 million in 2015 (Trading Economics, 2019). According to the statistics of the Investment Office in Turkey, Russia is among the top investors in Turkey especially between 2003-2017 period with 6.10% of the overall FDI inflows to Turkey.

6.2. Qualitative Analysis

6.2.1. Economic Sanctions Process and Outcomes for Each Country

6.2.1.a. Process and Outcomes for Russia

The quantitative data shows that Western sanctions have a negative impact on the trade relations with Turkey and Russia. The time series that was used in the regression was from 1992 to 2018. In this qualitative part the focus will be on the latest Western sanctions to Russia and to Turkey (after 2014). In 2014, Western world (the U.S. and the E.U) imposed sanctions against Russia after the annexation of Crimea and the tension in Ukraine. As we can recall the main aim of imposing sanctions or especially economic sanctions, which are related to imports/exports, tariffs, investment, is to change the behavior of the target country. The Western sanctions were imposed to change Russia's behavior, but the sender countries knew that Russia will not give Crimea back. Therefore, the main idea of the sender countries was just to put pressure on Russia to deter it from taking more aggressive role in the world. Russia's response to the imposed sanctions were retaliation. Russia from its side also imposed sanctions to the Western senders. Russian economy after 2014 period faced with a downfall where the GDP of Russia decreased from $2063.7 billion in 2014 to $1368.4 billion in 2015 (Trading Economics, 2019). This depreciation in the economy does not fully show that the sanctions reached their aim of putting economic pressure on Russia because there are some other factors that might affected the results. In the case of Russia this major factor would be the oil and gas prices. It has been known that Russian economy is mainly depending on oil and gas exports, which makes Russian economy vulnerable to any kind of volatility in the oil prices. As it can be seen from the Graph 3 below, the oil prices declined sharply starting from 2014 and the decline continued in 2015 reaching its bottom line in 2016.

Graph 3. Crude Oil (2009 - 2019)

Source: Trading Economics (Accessed on 16.04.2019)

Mainly the EU was the sender that targets Russia but last year in 2018 the U.S. take an active role in imposing sanctions to Russia because of Ukraine and additionally because of actions in Syria and 2016 U.S. presidential election.

When the first sanctions hit the Russian economy the strategy President Putin followed was to prioritize stability rather than economic growth. The long-term stability was and still is the priority of Putin rather than the growth. A finance specialist, Alexandre Abramov said that "Sanctions haven't broken the country's macroeconomic stability, but sanctions are cutting off the path to development. In terms of accelerating growth rates, enacting effective structural reforms — sanctions are sapping the country of these possibilities." (Troianovski, 2018). Therefore, the sanctions do not have an apparent impact on the economy but indirectly influence the way economic policies are settled. Also, the statistical data indicate that the stability is preserved during the years that Russia is under sanctions. For example, the inflation rate after 2014 the inflation rate in Russia started to increase from 7.8% to 15.6% in 2015, to decrease later to the level of 7% in 2016. In the next two years the inflation kept decreasing, in 2017 it was 3.7% and in 2018 it was 2.9%. This year, the inflation rate of Russia increased to 5.3% and become the highest since 2016 (Trading Economics, 2019). Another economic indicator that is important to understand whether Russia has been affected negatively by the sanctions is the unemployment rate. The unemployment rate is downward trending. In 2014 the unemployment rate was 5.16% and most probably after the sanctions in 2015 it slightly increased to 5.57%. It was almost the same in 2016 as well but after that in 2017 the unemployment rate decreased to 5.2% and in 2018 it has reached the level of 5.06% (The World Bank, 2019). According to the Central Bank of the Russian Federation Data, the international reserves started to decrease towards the end of 2014 (January: $498 Million, December: $385 Million) and kept decreasing in 2015 and 2016. But it increased in 2017 and 2018 and closely reached the level in 2014. The data on unemployment, inflation and international reserves displays that Russia, as Putin internalized, managed to preserve the stability of economic indicators. Russia's GDP growth rate has fallen below zero after 2014 hitting the level of -2.8% in 2015. In 2016 there was a slight improvement in the growth rate with it being -0.2%. In 2017, the growth rate steps up on zero level and reached 1.5% (The World Bank, 2019). Therefore, the sanctions prevented Russian economic growth to develop further which probably affected the middle class. However, by keeping other economic indicators such as inflation and unemployment relatively under control, Russia shows that the sanctions have limited effect on the economic stability.

Putin as well as prioritize economic stability during the sanctions, also gives importance to the economic independence (Prokopenko, 2018). To follow this goal Russia, due to the sanctions and low oil prices, started to save rather than spend. Even though sanctions have a negative effect on the economic growth, as an economist Lilit Gevorgyan says that the depreciation of Russian ruble has benefitted Russian exports since the energy companies sell their products in dollars while investing in rubles. Also, in 2014 the retaliation of Russia towards the economic sanctions from the West boosted agricultural production. This import substitution policy where Russia bans food imports from the West and starts to foster domestic production helped Russia to increase their food exports. According to the World Bank Report, Russia's export diversification is limited because the share of oil and gas products compose 59% of exports in 2017 (2018). Abramov, finance specialist, said that "Sanctions, strange as it may seem, steeled the economic wing of the government and taught them to act in sophisticated ways in very difficult situations," and Navalny's economic advisor Milov said that the sanctions will not collapse Russia's economy but because the economic sanctions work in the long-run the citizens must see that this is a dead end foreign policy (Troianovski, 2018).

In such a situation Russia uses its earnings from high oil prices to ease the pressure on the economy but on the other hand avoids better reforms that can promote better economy and attract more investors to the country. Even though Russia kept the inflation and unemployment under control, it cannot attract foreign investment to the country. The foreign investors anticipate the uncertainty and additional sanctions; therefore, they do not invest in Russia. Russian investors are not allowed to invest in EU and the partners from Asia or Arabia behave timid because of possible follow-up sanctions (Prokopenko, 2018). Therefore, Gevorgyan, asserts that because of underinvestment, missed business opportunities and slow modernization, the cost of Western sanction will be 0.2% in economic growth in the long-run (Troianovski, 2018).

In a way sanctions to Russia can be considered as failure because the West could not change the foreign policy of Russia in Ukraine or in Syria or in any other international situation with their economic sanctions. However, sanctions have put an economic pressure on Russia, even though it is not very obvious. Russia's dependence on oil prices and its immediate turn to domestic production has saved Russia from a big downfall but at the same time the volatility in oil prices affected Russia negatively. Another aspect that can be evaluated as a reason for failure is the reaction of the public in that target country. As explained by the literature, effective sanctions expect that the target country's people put political pressure on the authorities and demand a change in the foreign policy of the country. In the case of Russia, the surveys conducted by the Levada Center in 2017 shows that majority of the respondents believe that they should not adapt to the political position caused by the Western sanctions: 70% of the participants answered that Russia should follow its own political course, while 19% said that it is necessary to find a way to negotiate (Galanina, 2017). Even though the first sanctions were imposed in 2014, the public opinion on sanctions and their support for their government did not change. Russian citizens did not put political pressure on the authorities rather they showed their support for the government actions. Another survey which was conducted in 2018 by Levada Center shows that 42% of the respondents do not worry too much about Western sanctions while only 7% of them are very worried. 45% of the participants say that the Western sanctions did not create serious problems to them and to their family while only 3% of them say that Western sanctions caused very serious problems to them and their family. Other from these, we can also see the support of its citizens via the elections.

Putin's popularity increases without being influenced by any sanctions. In 2018, Putin won the presidential elections with 76% share of vote which shows that people are satisfied with the performance of institutions (Levada Center, April 2018).

6.2.1.b. Process and Outcomes for Turkey

The Western sanctions against Turkey has a different trajectory than the ones imposed on Russia. In Russian case we witnessed a retaliation and still the sanctions are extended by the West and it is an ongoing process. Nevertheless, in the case of Turkey we witnessed a retaliation first but then a negotiation with the U.S. which ended the sanctions.

When the U.S. first imposed sanctions against Turkey in 2018, it led to a serious depreciation of Turkish Lira. In August of 2018 the Dollar reached its highest level of 6.86 right after the sanctions. And the release of Pastor Brunson in October 2018 eased the tension between Turkey and the U.S. and ended the sanctions period, which resulted with a slight appreciation of Turkish Lira. Even though the lira was stabilized, as an economist Inan Demir said that government would reduce spending and the central bank would raise borrowing costs (Ant, 2018). Furthermore, not only the currency but also the GDP growth rate has affected by the US economic sanctions imposed on Turkey in Q3. As shown in the Graph 4, GDP in Turkey contracted in the third and fourth quarters of 2018. In Q3 it contracted 1.6% while in Q4 it contracted 2.4%. This apparent decline can be associated to the economic sanctions.

Graph 4. GDP Growth Rate of Turkey Quarterly 2018

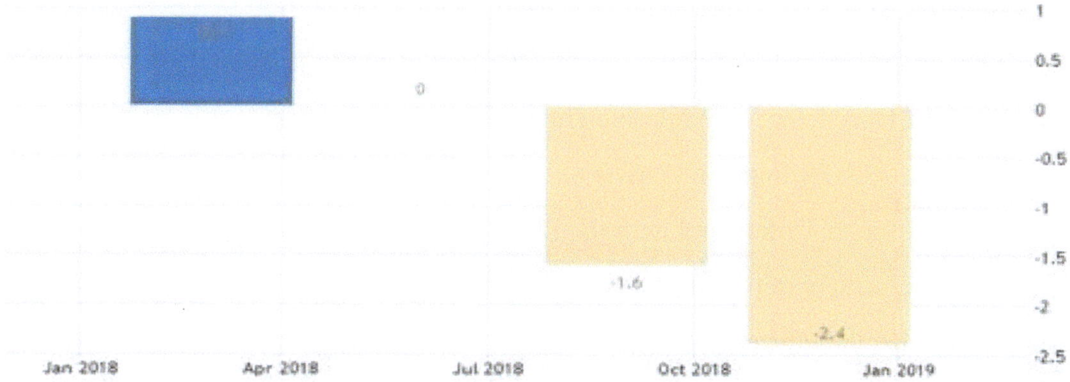

Source: Trading Economics (Accessed 30.04.2019)

In last round of the economic sanctions from the U.S., Ankara refused to negotiate by not releasing pastor Brunson. With further depreciation of the lira, Turkey estranged from its Western allies and started to look for an affiliation with Russia.

While USD appreciate against the TRY, EUR also increase in value against lira after the economic sanctions and reached 7.74 in September. The Turkish economic crisis because of the sanctions has given the opportunity to the E.U. to reevaluate the dominance of dollar. Europe is one of the main trading partners of Turkey and Turkey is the 4th biggest export market and 5th largest import provider of EU (European Commission, 2019). Since the Eu is the main trading partner of Turkey, it supported Turkey against the US economic sanctions. In the previous section I presented how German chancellor and Italian Minister backed Turkey. This shows that Turkey and the EU has economic interdependence and EU takes sides with Turkey against US for domineering a trade partner. In this direction, European Parliament announced that the problem between Turkey and the U.S. should be solved with "constructive diplomatic engagement" and Germany's foreign minister Heiko Maas criticized the sanctions by saying that "Washington's sanctions policy forces us Europeans to formulate a response. Because it is affecting us, Germany and Europe, when the U.S. abruptly and unilaterally imposing often unspecified sanctions against Russia, China, Turkey and maybe in the future against our other important trading partners," and further he suggested to "strengthen the autonomy and sovereignty of Europe in the fields of trade, economy and finance policies," which will reduce the U.S. supremacy in global finance (Hurriyet Daily News, 2018). Additionally, the economy minister of France declared that they will establish economic ties with Turkey, which also indicates that France is taking the side of Turkey against the U.S. (Süsler, 2018).

After the reaction that EU presented after the sanctions against Turkey, the US side called the EU as a foe. Apparently, Trump administration was not happy with this counter response. But by imposing tariffs on steel and aluminum US inflicted damage to the economic ties with Turkey and with the EU. The UK leaving the EU has affected the EU economy negatively and with the threats of raising import taxes on European cars aggravate the tension between the Us and the Eu. To decrease the dominance of the US, the EU and Turkey stick together in economic issues. President Trump's decisions foreign policy towards the EU and Turkey has increased the ambition in both countries to converge in terms of trade and foreign policy.

In the first wave of economic sanctions against Turkey and the depreciation of Turkish lira affected the economy negatively, but not the government. Turkish society supported the decision of not releasing the pastor and not negotiating with the U.S. After Turkish economy went bad to worse, the people demanded a change in the policies of the government and suggested a betterment in the relations with the U.S. to ease the economic pressure. Initially, according to the surveys of Optimar Research Company, the public supported Turkish foreign policy at a time when the US sanctions targeting the domestic economy (Sudagezer, 2018). Furthermore, the Optimar research indicates that 74.5% of the population believes that the US has put political pressure on Turkey over dollars, and 73.5% of respondents supported Turkey's trade with lira to reduce the impact of the dollar. Also, a great majority of the respondents positively considers the arrest of Pastor Brunson. While in the first period of the sanction the public opinion supports Turkish government another research after the sanctions presents how people think about politics, economics, Turkey and international agenda.

According to the Research on Social-Political Trends in Turkey (TSSEA) research, people place rising unemployment and high cost of living on the top of their list of problems. 57.1% of the participants state that their economic well-being worsened in the recent year, while 21.9% of them state that they have not affected by economic developments. According to the survey government's economic policies that people consider as successful decreased by 14.2 points in 2018 (CTRS, 2019). The results of the survey interpret that the worsening economy lead to less political support. As along with the normal institutional evolution when public is not satisfied with the policies, the government loses their political support from its citizens. Economic instability in Turkey resulted with declining political support towards the current government in Turkey. Based on the survey conducted in December 2018, we cannot fully confirm that economic sanctions lead such results, but we can indirectly indicate that the US sanctions has added economic problems on Turkish economy. After sanctions strike the people economically, their concerns and their reaction toward the government changed.

Allen (2005) suggested that for sanctions to be effective the sender country impose economic costs on the public of the target country and in turn the public exert pressure on the government to change its foreign policy. Therefore, here we see that the economic sanctions worked because the people who hit by the economic sanctions demand a political change from its government. Referring to the literature, the US imposed economic sanctions to bring about a change not only in the attitude towards Brunson but also in political behavior (Allen, 2005). Since the US imposed sanctions on many other countries as well, this shows that it struggles to prove that US dollar and the US as a country dominates the international politics and economics.

6.2.1.c. Assessment of Sanctions on Russia and Turkey

I analyzed and shows the process and outcomes of the economic sanctions against Russia and Turkey. The trajectory of both countries has differences in terms of the process and the completion. If we revoke from the literature review, the studies showed that economic sanctions work better if they target an ally than an adversary. This is because allies have stronger economic ties and has the possibility of interdependency in terms of trade while adversaries have less economic and political ties with each other. If we apply this to cases of Russia and Turkey, it can be deduced that it is accurate. Even though the West (EU and US) has economic ties with Russia, still they do not consider each other as an ally, however, the West and Turkey has economic ties and Turkey is considered as an ally. Turkey is an ally because of NATO and also for a long time Turkey desires to be a member of the EU. Therefore, when we see that Western economic sanctions on Russia did not have an obvious result and Russia still endures the economic pressure, it can be said that it is because Russia did not receive a blow from an ally. In Turkish case, since Turkey is one of the main trading partners with the US (4th largest source of import and 5th largest source of export), the economic sanctions influenced Turkey adversely. Leaving Turkey with a depreciated currency, slowed down growth rate and more.

Another detail that the analysis of economic sanctions process revealed is the reaction of public towards the response of their government to the sanctions. Turkish people, first applauded Erdogan but then put political pressure on the Turkish government to change their behavior towards the US because the economy was going worse. And eventually, Erdogan released pastor Brunson and negotiated with the US. However, in the case of Russia, the sources indicate that the public did not force Russia to change its foreign policy. This can be confirmed through electoral results as well. Russian citizens continue to support their government while economic climate in Turkey made less significant victory for the current government in the elections. Russian economy also contracted after the sanctions, but I think because oil and gas exports sustain its economy, public in Russia did not act like Turkish people.

6.2.2. Bilateral Trade Between Russia and Turkey

In order to figure out the trade between Russia and Turkey I used several indexes that will help me to analyze the trade patterns. Those indexes are revealed comparative advantage index, trade complementarity index and trade intensity index. Here, I will be referring to the data presented in the results section of the thesis. Revealed comparative advantage (RCA) a significant index to evaluate the export potential of a country. To have a better understanding of the index and as a follow up to the quantitative part of the thesis, I decided to include the top traded good between Russia and Turkey as some of the products. That way, we will see in which top traded goods Turkey or Russia has the comparative advantage. Also, main product groups such as capital goods, consumer goods, intermediate goods and raw materials were included in the tables.

According to the Table 3, Turkey has 'revealed' comparative advantage over Russia in terms of vegetable, textile and clothing and raw materials. Since, the values for these products have always been bigger than 1 over the years, safely this judgement can be made. The RCA values for consumer goods, intermediate goods and metals changed over time, displaying both less and higher values from the breaking point (1). In terms of fuels, Turkey has an obvious comparative disadvantage over Russia and accordingly the values are less than 1 throughout the whole period. The RCA values for capital goods indicates that Turkey had a slight 'revealed' comparative advantage in 1996 and 1997 but after that the values drop below 1, turning into a comparative disadvantage. In Table 4, Russia has 'revealed' comparative advantage over Turkey in term of fuels and metals. Since, the values for these products have always been bigger than 1 over the years, safely this judgement can be made. The RCA values for consumer goods, intermediate goods, raw materials and vegetables changed over time, displaying both less and higher values from the breaking point (1). In terms of textile and clothing and capital goods, Russia has an obvious comparative disadvantage over Turkey and accordingly the values are less than 1 throughout the whole period. The RCA values for vegetables indicates that Russia had a 'revealed' comparative disadvantage from 1997 until 2008 but after 2011 the values step up on 1, turning into a comparative advantage, but still the Russia's RCA for vegetables are less than Turkey's RCA for vegetables.

The following index is trade complementarity index (TCI) which displays whether the export pattern of one country matches with the import pattern of its partner. According to the Table 5, the trade complementarity index values between Russia and Turkey are high (over 50) in the period of 2011-2017. Therefore, I can say that the Russia and Turkey are highly complementary of each other and both have strong bilateral trade. After 2014 the value of TCI decreased from 63 to 60 in 2015, which can be explained again with the economic policy changes of Russia after Western sanctions. In, 2016 the value dropped to 59 because of the Russian sanctions against Turkey in 2015. As one can recall, the exposed economic sanctions on Turkey have limited the trade between Russia and Turkey until recently.

The last index is trade intensity index (TII), which compares the trade between two countries over their average trade with the world. The Table 6 and the Graph 1 present that the trade between Russia and Turkey has always been higher than their trade with the world on average. After 2014 the TII value decreased from 2.41 to 2.25 in 2015 which can be explained with the sanctions against Russia. From 2015 to 2016 the TII value declined again from 2.25 to 1.09 which is a very big decline for these two countries, and this can be explained with the 2015 plane crisis between Russia and Turkey where they imposed sanctions against each other. After hitting the bottom in 2016, in 2017 the value started to increase from 1.09 to 1.34 in 2017.

In brief, the trade indexes that I used to investigate the bilateral trade between Russia and Turkey indicate that the two countries have intense bilateral trade and their products are generally complementary. Therefore, they use their comparative advantage wisely when it comes to trade. From an IPE perspective, we know that comparative advantage is a part of liberal thought where economists believed that if each country specialize in what they are good at will result with a win-win for everyone trading. In the case of Russia, it exports fuels and metals because it has clear revealed comparative advantage on these products. On the contrary, Turkey exports vegetable, clothes and raw materials in which it has comparative advantage.

6.2.3. Trade Diversification of Russia and Turkey

One of the key issues in this study is the trade diversification which comes out as a part of bilateral trade and/or a response to economic sanctions. Trade diversification has two components in this study, export diversification and commercial diversification.

Deducing from the concept of diversification, which is simply a way to minimize the risks, by investing in many options rather than sticking to one, commercial diversification can be defined as a country's search for new trade partners to decrease risk of a possible crisis and its negative impacts on itself. In the case of sanctions, generally target countries either retaliate or negotiate with the sender country. Alongside with one of these options I believe that target country can search for a new trade partner while retaliating to alleviate the economic pressure by exporting to the new partner or import the restricted commodities from it. Also, it can search for new trade partners before or after negotiating with the sender country just to reduce the dependence on the sender country's trade in case of a new crisis between those two.

Some of the researches detect evidence for trade diversion rather than trade diversification while investigating the influence of economic sanctions on bilateral trade of certain countries. For example; Haidar (2016) search for the impacts of sanctions on exports of Iran. His results present evidence for trade diversion and further he shows that bigger portion (two-thirds) of export value diverted from sender country to non-sender countries. Early (2009) discovered that sanctions may motivate allies of sanction sender country to increase their trade with the target country, to decrease the impact of economic sanctions. Early also came to conclusion that third countries decide to help the target counties by commercial interests rather than political interests. Notwithstanding, one of the main findings of Haidar's (2016) study was that the new partners of trade are more politically-friendly with the target country. In other words, the emergence of trade diversion in economically sanctioned countries seem to be grounded on political reasons rather than strictly economic or commercial arguments. In this sense, it is fundamental to analyze the pre-existing political relations of target countries in order to account for the existence of trade diversion.

In the case of Turkey, as expected, the trade between the sender country and the target country decreases due to the economic sanctions, the last graph also shows that the trade between the US and Turkey was increasing until 2017 but after the sanctions the trade slightly decreased. However, I showed what European leaders and Russian officials said about the economic sanctions imposed against Turkey. The EU criticism of US policy towards its ally, Turkey, shows that EU as another ally of the US, supports Turkey and give green light for further stronger economic ties with it. The EU with a liberal approach draws a line between economics and politics because US sanctions shows a conflict of interest rather than harmony of interests between free countries. The EU criticized the US because they know that limiting the free exchange of goods and lowering the level of benefits will worsen the mutual trade between many countries, which might lead to wars.

Furthermore, I can say that the sanctions against Turkey brought the EU and Turkey closer in terms of economic trade partnership. According to the TUIK data, the exports of Turkey to EU, Germany, France and Italy have increased prominently from 2017 to 2018 which also proves that the trade between the European countries and Turkey has increased after the US sanctions (*cf. Figure 2*, page 80). The first graph shows the Turkish exports to France, in 2016 and 2017 the export amount was almost equal around \$6 billion but in 2018 it increased to \$7 billion. Second graph for Turkish exports to Germany indicates a rising trend in the exports. Especially the trade increased in 2018, which again may be due to the Germany's support to Turkey after it was exposed to US sanctions. Likely, the third graph, Turkey exports to Italy, has the same trend as the other European countries. Turkey exports to the EU in general clearly displays the increase and cooperation of Turkey and the EU. In 2017 Turkish exports approximately were worth \$73 billion, but in 2018 this number increased to \$84 billion. The first four graphs prove that Turkish export to the EU, especially to the states that supported Turkey against the US has increased. The growing trade relations with the EU after the sanctions also shows that the ally of the sanction sender country increase its trade with the target country to decrease the economic impact of the economic sanctions. Therefore, Turkey is not only using trade diversification as a tool to alleviate the pressure, but also Turkey is performing trade diversion by having better trade relations with the allies of the sanction sender country.

Not only with the allies of the sender country but also other third countries help the target country to lessen the effect of economic sanctions by commercial interests. President Erdogan on August 2018 said that "Before it is too late, Washington must give up the misguided notion that our relationship can be asymmetrical and come to terms with the fact that Turkey has alternatives," (Pamuk, 2018). Further he kept stressing on the alternatives by "Failure to reverse this trend of unilateralism and disrespect will require us to start looking for new friends and allies," (Baykan, 2018). Estranged from the US, Turkey started to shift to trade in national currencies starting with Russia, Ukraine and China. On 10th of August 2018, Putin and Erdogan had a telephone conversation with each other. On the phone the presidents discussed the current issues and future economic cooperation in terms of trade between Russia and Turkey. They evaluated positively that both countries implement joint strategic projects especially in energy sector (President of Russia, 2018). This was no surprise that Russia and Turkey, the big powers of the Eurasian region, back one another in the case of the sanctions that were imposed on both of them. Foreign minister Lavrov uttered that the US sanctions to both Russia and Turkey were improper policy and a way to earn an unjust comparative advantage in international trade (Reuters, 2018). This is a way of saying that both of these countries have experienced same kind of unfair punishment from the West and they will support each other. While Turkey started to export more to the EU and diverse its trade, also we can see that Turkey diversify towards Russia. The fifth graph shows Turkey exports to Russia and from 2017 to 2018 there is an obvious increase in the export amount. Since, Russia is not an ally of the US, I cannot consider this increased trade relation as trade diversion. Even though Russia took such a supportive stand towards Turkey, their trade relations did not increase compatibly with the statements. The increase in the trade relations cannot be considered as extreme. The reason for a slight increase can be because both countries were hit by the sanctions, and Russia imposed sanctions on Turkey in 2015. However still after the US sanctions against Turkey, Russia showed its support and the cooperation between these two countries increased, and the political relations are tighter between those two countries.

Figure 2. Turkey Exports to France, Germany, Italy, EU, Russia and US 2014 - 2018

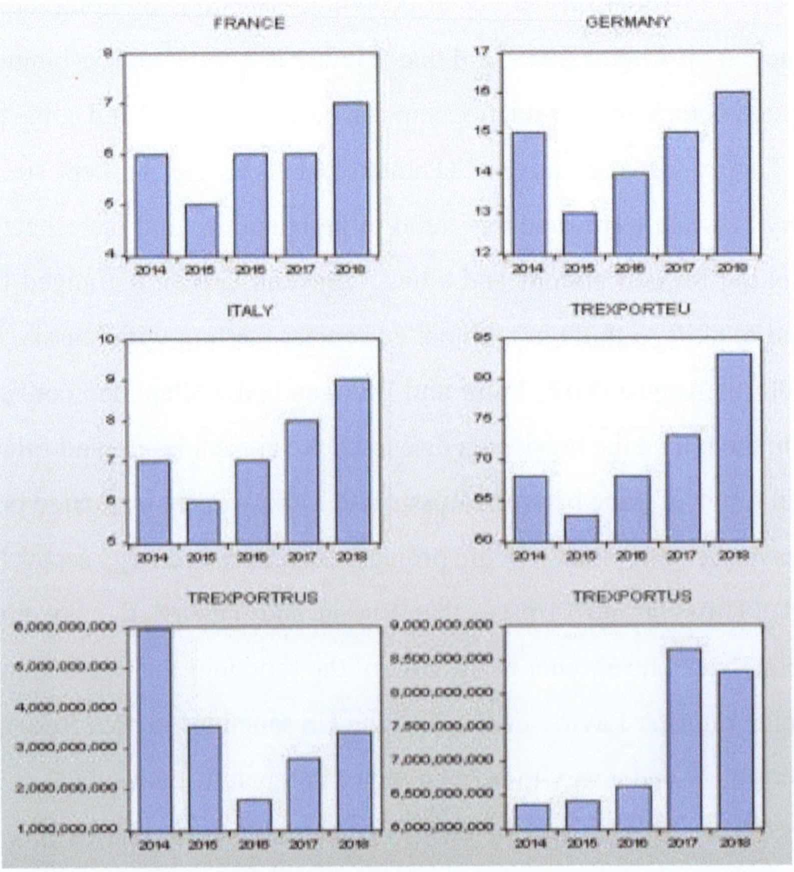

Source: Data taken from TUIK. Constructed by the author.

In the case of Russia, after the Western sanction in 2014, the country had a more protective economic policy where it used protectionism and import substitution. This protective policy orientation shows Russia's nationalist response to sanctions. Modern nationalists also argue that in trade exports should be encouraged while imports should be limited. Russia protects its local economy with interventionist policies because according to nationalists a country's wealth and strength depend on trade surplus. Therefore, Russia to keep its powerful state image against the West use protective economic policy as a response.

Import substitution has encouraged domestic production and replacement of imported goods with the domestic ones, which means that protectionism limited the importation of goods. Therefore, statistically in the first two or three years we see that the Russia's imports from sanctioning or non-sanctioning countries decreased. The director of the department of the development of economic sectors, Alexander Maslennikov, evaluated the imposed food embargo on certain goods from the West as a part of import substitution program as successful catalyst for domestic agricultural producers and further suggested that Russia's exports of food and agriculture increased by 6% (Ministry of Economic Development of Russia, 2017). Maslennikov in the interview with Regions of Russia, said that by import substitution they are protecting their development and growth, but they are not planning to abandon imports from other countries or replacing them with domestic ones (2017).

On the other hand, as discussed for Turkey, after the Western sanctions, Russia's exports to the EU decreased after 2014 until increasing again starting from 2017. The same patterns apply for the Russia's imports from the EU. Because of the economic sanctions and reciprocal restrictive measures, the decrease in trade was expected. However, Russia deflect its direction towards Asia and Central Asia. Right after the Western sanctions, in 2014 Russia and China has signed a gas deal worth $400 billion, where Russia will export gas to China for the next 30 years (Bond and Korteweg, Centre for European Reform, 2014). Putin signed an agreement aiming Chinese-Russian cooperation in energy sector and delineating the route for natural gas supplies on October 2014 (President of Russia, 2015). In 2014, Russia and China discussed the project to develop gas supply infrastructure that enables gas exports to China. Further signed the agreement to construct gas pipeline (President of Russia, 2014). Also, both countries have signed various agreements to strengthen economic relations with each other. In one of the agreements Sberbank opened a 6-billion-yuan credit line with China Development Bank. In 2014, Putin signed an agreement which states that BRICS countries will provide financial support to any of their partners in case of a dollar liquidity problem in their national financial system (President of Russia, 2015). In 2015 China and Russia avoid double taxation and prevent tax evasion aiming to develop mutual cooperation and attract mutual investments (President of Russia, 2016). Other than China, Russia also begin to increase its bilateral relations with Pakistan via trade and cooperation in overcoming terrorism. In Pakistan's accession to Shanghai Cooperation Organization (SCO) in 2015, both countries uttered the importance of each other for their foreign policy, and they make effort to increase the trade and economic ties (President of Russia, 2015).

Right after the Western sanctions on Russia, Eurasian Economic Union (EAEU) treaty was signed in May 2014. Russia with other countries in the region such as Kazakhstan, Kyrgyzstan, Armenia and Belarus created this international organization for regional economic integration (EAEU, 2019). Russia's attempt to create an alternative to its Western trade partners right after the sanctions asserts that it searched for alternatives and diversified its commercial partners. This regional economic cooperation that entered into force in 2015 aimed to provide "free movement of goods, services, capital and labor, pursues coordinated, harmonized and single policy in the sectors determined by the Treaty and international agreements within the Union" (EAEU, 2019). According to the statistical data provided in EAEU's official webpage, the graphs indicating export, import and trade balance from 2016 and 2018 show the increase in export numbers in each member-state (*cf. Figure 3 and 4*, page 83). Even though the balance of trade is negative in all the member-states except Belarus, in general the officials of countries suggest that this regional union contributed to mutual development. Alexander Yakovlev, the trade representative of Russia in Kazakhstan, in an interview says that establishing EAEU was appropriate and convenient, also it benefits all the participants (Dzhilkishinova, 2018). Consequently, Russia after the sanctions took due precautions domestically and diversified its trade towards its regional partners through Eurasian Economic Union and towards Asia especially increasing trade with China. Even though the trade between Russia and Turkey increased especially in 2018, Russia has given priority to neighboring countries and the economic giants of Asia. From the IPE perspective, again, we see the nationalist response of Russia to the sanctions. By prioritizing its national interests and power, Russia verge to its third country allies to counterbalance the effects of economic sanctions.

Figure 3: Export and import of services for EAEU member-states 2016 - 2017 (million USD)

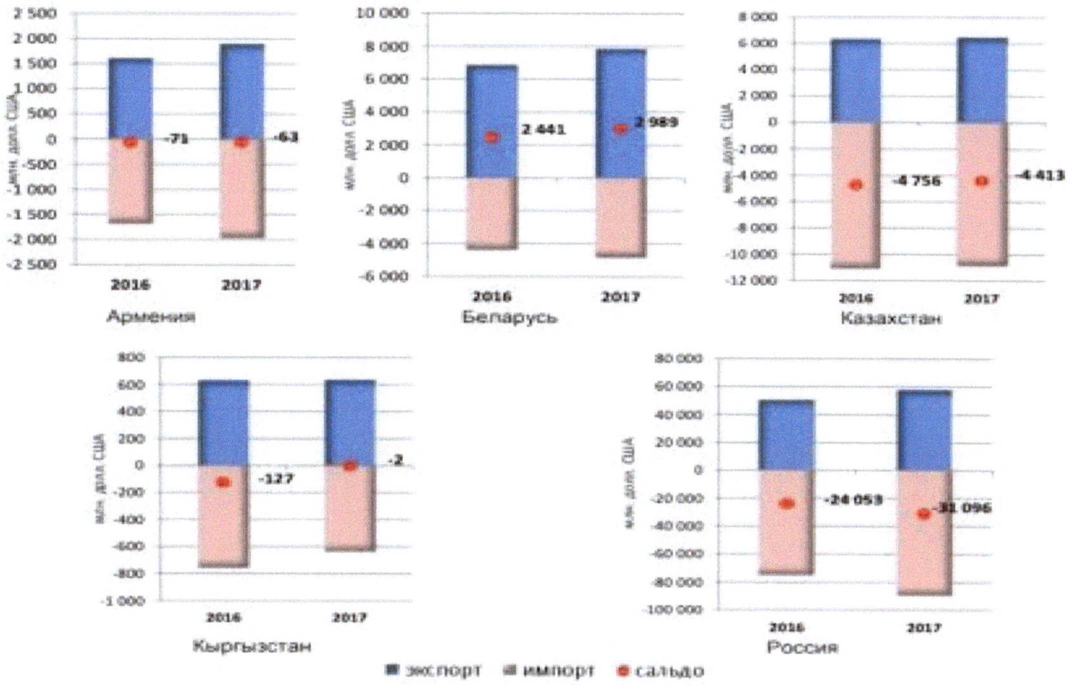

Source: EAEU Statistics. (Accessed 29.04.2019)

Figure 4: Exports, imports and balance of trade in services for EAEU member-states 2017 - 2018 (million USD)

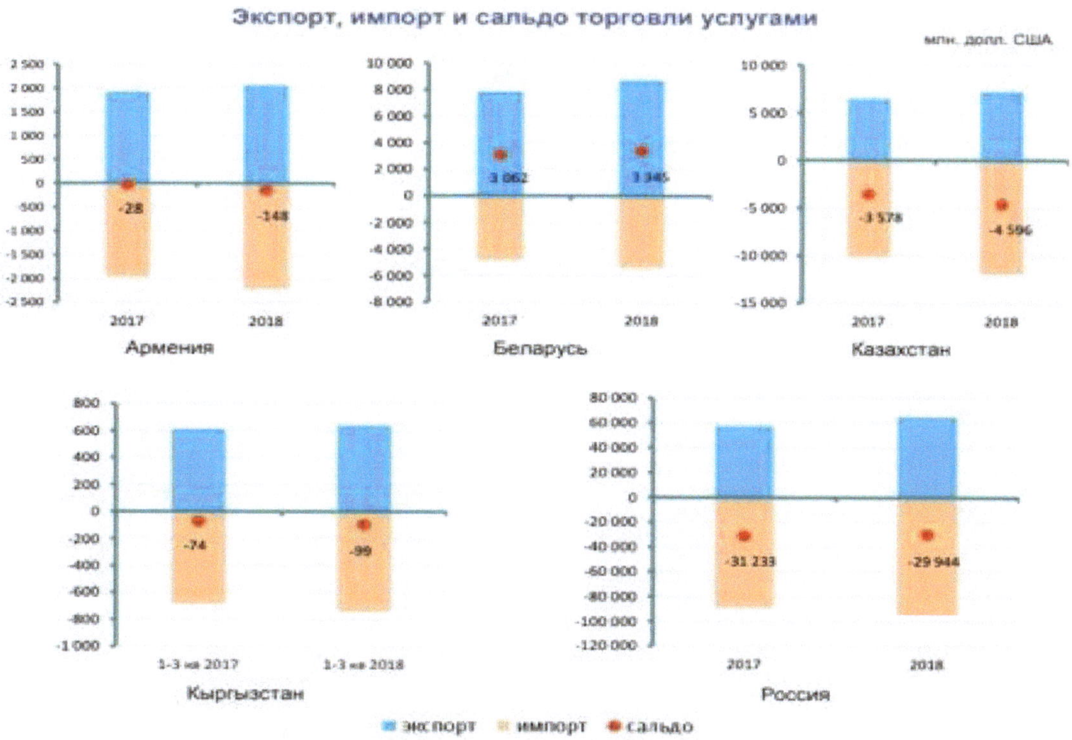

Source: EAEU Statistics. (Accessed 29.04.2019)

CHAPTER 7: SUMMARY & CONCLUSION

This study aimed to find an answer to the research question "How did Western economic sanctions reshaped the bilateral trade between Russia and Turkey?". The impacts on economic sanctions is a relevant topic today since a lot of countries and international organizations use sanctions as a foreign policy tool and as an alternative to war. While this study was organized Turkey was freshly exposed to economic sanctions from the US and the West added new sanctions to the list of already existing sanctions on Russia. In the not too distant past having the sanctions in two of the countries that are in my field of interest made this study relevant.

In order to analyze the research problem of impacts of economic sanctions and the responses to them, I conducted an explanatory sequential mixed method design. In the first part I investigated my first hypothesis "Economic sanctions imposed on two target countries that already have trade relations will increase the bilateral trade between them" by quantitative analysis. The analysis was carried out with a logarithmic regression with time series in the period of 1992 to 2018. The main findings of the logarithmic regression indicated that GDP of Turkey, GDP of Russia and Western sanctions against Turkey have positive impact on the bilateral trade between Russia and Turkey. When the same logarithmic regressions were applied to the selected traded goods between Russia and Turkey, the results again show that there is a positive impact of sanctions in the trade of metals between two countries. Deducing from these results the H1 was partially proven. It is not fully accepted because the results did not indicate any meaningful outcomes for impact of sanctions against Russia on bilateral trade. This was unexpected since I thought that Western sanctions on both countries would push them closer in terms of economic relations. Having no meaningful result might indicate that Russia's bilateral trade influenced by the GDP and other variables which were not included in this regression.

As a follow-up to the quantitative phase, I continued with qualitative analysis. The analysis was carried out with content analysis of many official documents of agreements, projects and cooperation as well as trade indexes. This phase focused more on the responses to the economic sanctions between 2014 and 2018 and enlarged upon the bilateral trade between Russia and Turkey between 1992-2018. The hypothesis of qualitative part was "The bigger the share of the sender in the target, the more target country will need to diversify to alleviate the pressure of economic sanctions". The main findings of the analysis prove that H2 was true. Both Russia and Turkey after they were exposed to sanctions diversified their trade by searching for alternative commercial partners.

One of the unexpected results was that the qualitative analysis also showed the differences between Russia and Turkey in terms of process and outcomes of sanctions. Russia preferred to retaliate and imposed counter sanctions since 2014, the foreign policy and economic policies of Russian government gained public acceptance. On the other side, Turkey decided to retaliate to the US economic sanctions with counter-sanctions as well. However, the depreciation of Turkish lira, the increase in inflation, unemployment and cost of living bothered Turkish citizens. The rising economic concerns among the society led the government to reevaluate their policies. Turkish government, which felt political pressure in the event of a possible loss of votes in upcoming elections, changed its foreign policy and chose to negotiate with the US. Therefore, the economic sanctions have negative impacts on the target countries but in Turkish case sanctions were successful since it changed the behavior of Turkey. In the Russian case I can suggest that it is not either successful or unsuccessful. Russian sanctions did affect the economy negatively but mostly it was because of the indirect effect of decline in oil prices. Also, the sanctions have not led any public reaction towards the Russian government demanding a change in the foreign policy. Because Russia still follows its own policies and gets support from its citizens the sanctions cannot be considered fully successful.

Another unexpected result was finding that sanctions against Russia had no statistically meaningful impact on the bilateral trade between Russia and Turkey. This result deduced from the regression, examined in detail in the qualitative part by trade indexes, trade agreements and other documents. The qualitative results suggest that the bilateral trade between Russia and Turkey decreased after 2014 especially decreased after unfortunate plane crisis between these two countries in 2015. However, the trade increased after the political tension between the two were solved in 2016 and it kept increasing after Turkey was exposed to Western economic sanctions. Moreover, Russia increased its trade with Central Asian and Asian countries right after 2014 sanctions while Turkey increased its trade with the EU countries after sanctions in 2018. Thus, Russia and Turkey in terms of trade are an alternative for their Western trade partners however they are not the first choice of each other.

Since economic and political relations are so interconnected with each other, to explain the impacts of economic sanctions on bilateral trade between countries I made use of international political economy theories. Two of the main IPE theories, liberalism and nationalism, provide an insight to better understand the liberal aims of economic sanctions and nationalistic responses to them. In the case of sanctions imposed on Russia, sanctions hold liberal aims to create peace and order without causing a war while sanctions against Turkey hold nationalistic aims as an addition to the liberal ones. Judging from this, the responses to the sanctions show more nationalistic features where target countries try to keep their power against the sender and look for alternative countries to serve their national interests. Moreover, by using liberal tools such as free trade and comparative advantage, the target countries give a nationalist response to sanctions. Also, as one of the main findings of the thesis, trade diversion is a concept where nationalism and liberalism are interbedded. Turkey is performing trade diversion by having better trade relations with the allies of the sanction sender country which again asserts target countries' liberal moves with nationalist intentions.

This study has addressed many gaps in the literature in terms of content, case selection, design, and arguments. The literature of economic sanctions is broad and generally, researchers used large N samples or focused on only one case. In this study, I focused on two recently sanctioned countries, Russia and Turkey. Russia is one of the most popular cases when studying economic sanctions while recent Western sanctions against Turkey has not been studied. Many studies investigated the bilateral trade between the sender and the target country while I looked at two target countries and interaction with each other after the sanctions. Researchers either preferred to use quantitative or qualitative analysis but not both of them. But I thought that the mixed method was the best way to explain a topic of IPE since the field itself is mixed. As stated in the literature review, the literature is filled with studies showing the interest of sending countries but not including the target country's perspective. However, the subjects of this study are two target countries that examined the responses of them to the sanctions.

This research addressed to a very topical subject of economic sanctions and bilateral trade with the focus on Russia and Turkey. Economic sanctions are an ongoing process for Russia and have not solved yet for Turkey in the beginning of this study, makes this study have a very relevant and current topic. Therefore, this study helped to understand the contemporary economic and political relations between Russia and Turkey including their current relationship with the West. Based on this study, relevant authorities and persons can deduce possible impacts of economic sanctions and recent bilateral cooperation on international economic relations in the region.

As a final remark, this paper was based on the economic sanctions against Russia and Turkey from which many can benefit. However, it could be beneficial to change the cases and apply the design to the other target countries to see how sanctions affected their trade relations and their responses to the sanctions. Optionally, future research might work with a larger time series including years from the very past to examine older sanctions and their outcomes and as a result could set a theory. Additionally, future researchers can consider changing the theoretical approach by only focusing on economics or political science.

List of Sources

- Afesorgbor, S. K., & Mahadevan, R. (2016). The Impact of Economic Sanctions on Income Inequality of Target States. *AARHUS BSS.*
- Al, A. (2015). Politika-Ekonomi Kesişmesi: Yeni Bir Bilim Dalı Olarak Uluslararası Politik Ekonomi. *İGÜSBD*, *2*(1).
- Allen, S. H. (2005). The Determinants of Economic Sanctions Success and Failure. *International Interactions*, *31*(2), 117-138.
- Altan, M. (2013). Uluslararası Ekonomi Politik. *Anadolu Üniversitesi.*
- Ant, O. (2018). Turkey's Fast-Paced GDP Growth Shows Signs of Slowdown Ahead. In *Bloomberg*. Retrieved from https://www.bloomberg.com/news/articles/2018-09-10/turkey-gdp-grows-5-2-percent-in-second-quarter-meeting-estimate
- Attack on Ambassador Karlov is a Clear Provocation against Turkey-Russia Relations (2016). In *Presidency of the Republic of Turkey*. Retrieved from https://www.tccb.gov.tr/en/news/542/66432/buyukelci-karlova-duzenlenen-saldiri-turk-rus-iliskilerine-yonelik-acik-bir-provokasyon
- Aung San Suu Kyi Quotes. (n.d.). Retrieved May 1, 2019, from https://www.brainyquote.com/quotes/aung_san_suu_kyi_291374
- Barbieri, K. (2002). The Liberal Illusion: Does Trade Promote Peace? *University of Michigan Press*,
- Baykan, D. (2018, August 11). Erdogan warns US of harming its own interests, security. Retrieved April 10, 2019, from https://www.aa.com.tr/en/economy/erdogan-warns-us-of-harming-its-own-interests-security/1228138
- Berg, V., Hendrik, & Lewer, J. (2006), International Trade and Economic Growth, *M E Sharpe.*
- Bhojani, F., & Zengerle, P. (2017). Factbox: What do the new U.S. sanctions on Russia target? In *Reuters*. Retrieved from https://www.reuters.com/article/us-usa-trump-russia-sanctions-factbox/factbox-what-do-the-new-u-s-sanctions-on-russia-target-idUSKBN1AL0K1

- Bond, I., & Korteweg, R. (2014). Russia' Gas Deal with China: Business is Busines. In *Centre for European Union*. Retrieved from https://www.cer.eu/insights/russias-gas-deal-china-business-business
- Brady, L. J. (1987). The utility of economic sanctions as a policy instrument. *St. Martin's Press*.
- Brenton, P., Newfarmer, R., & Walkenhorst, P. (2007). Export Diversification: A Policy Portfolio Approach. *Yale University*.
- Çakmak, C., & Ustaoğlu, M. (2017). *Politics vs. trade: A Realist view on Turkish–Israeli economic relations* (Vol. 23). Israel Affairs. doi:10.1080/13537121.2016.1274506
- Caruso, R. (2003). The Impact of International Economic Sanctions on Trade: An Empirical Analysis. *Peace Economics, Peace Science, and Public Policy*, *9*(2).
- Caselli, F., Koren, M., Lisickly, M., & Tenreyro, S. (2015). Diversification Through Trade. *NBER Working Paper*.
- Cattaneo, O. (2007), Promoting Diversification and Exports in the Tourism Sector – Lessons from Mauritius, Zambia and Nigeria, *The World Bank*.
- Ceremony marking the completion of TurkStream gas pipeline's offshore section (2018). In *President of Russia*. Retrieved from http://en.kremlin.ru/events/president/news/59152
- Ceremony to mark the joining of the Power of Siberia gas pipeline's first section. (2014, September 01). Retrieved March 30, 2019, from http://en.kremlin.ru/catalog/countries/CN/events/46527
- Council of the European Union. (2017, October 23). EU restrictive measures in response to the crisis in Ukraine. Retrieved April 16, 2019, from https://www.consilium.europa.eu/en/policies/sanctions/ukraine-crisis/
- Cox, R. W. (1983). Gramsci, Hegemony and International Relations: An Essay in Method. *Millenium: Journal of International Studies*, *12*(2).
- Creswell, J. W. (2014). *Research Design Qualitative, Quantitative and Mixed Methods Approaches* (4thth ed.). N.p.: SAGE.
- CTRS. (2019). Türkiye Sosyal-Siyasal Eğilimler Araştırması 2018 Sonuçları. Retrieved April 27, 2019, from http://ctrs.khas.edu.tr/post/34/turkiye-sosyal-siyasal-egilimler-arastirmasi-2018-sonuclari

- Cumhurbaşkanlığı Sözcüsü Kalın: ABD'nin talepte bulunması kabul edilemez (2018). In *CNN Türk*. Retrieved from https://www.cnnturk.com/turkiye/cumhurbaskanligi-sozcusu-kalin-abdnin-talepte-bulunmasi-kabul-edilemez
- Daoudi, M.S., Dajani, M.S. (1983). Economic Sanctions: Ideals and Experience. *Routledge and Kegan Paul*.
- Dashti-Gibson, J., Davis, P., & Radecliff, B. (1997). On the Deter- minants of the Success of Economic Sanctions: An Empirical Analysis. *American Journal of Political Science*, *41*(2), 608-618.
- Databases (2019). In *TÜİK*. Retrieved from http://tuik.gov.tr/PreTabloArama.do?metod=search&araType=vt
- Dessy, S., Mbiekop, F., & Pallage, S. (2010), On the Mechanics of Trade-Induced Structural Transformation, *Journal of Macroeconomics* 32(1).
- Dizaji, S. F., & van Bergeijk, P. A. (2013). Potential early phase success and ultimate failure of economic sanctions: A VAR approach with an application to Iran. *Journal of Peace Research*, *50*(6), 721-726.
- Dong, Y., & Li, C. (2018). Economic sanction games among the US, the EU and Russia: Payoffs and potential effects. *Economic Modelling*, *73*, 117-128.
- Downe-Wamboldt, B. (1992). Content analysis: Method, applications, and issues. *Health Care for Women International*, *13*, 313-321.
- Drezner, D. Sanctions Sometimes Smart: Targeted Sanctions in Theory and Practice. *International Studies Review*, *13*.
- Drezner, D. W. (1999). The Sanctions Paradox Economic Statecraft and International Relations. *Cambridge University Press*.
- Drezner, D. W. (2003). Review: How Smart Are Smart Sanctions? *JSTOR*, *5*(1).
- Drezner, D. W. (2003). The Hidden Hand of Economic Coercion. *IO Foundation*, *57*(3).
- Dzhilkishinova, M. (2018, November 07). Kazakh-Russian economic cooperation is strong and developing, says Russian trade rep in Kazakhstan. Retrieved April 27, 2019, from https://astanatimes.com/2018/11/kazakh-russian-economic-cooperation-is-strong-and-developing-says-russian-trade-rep-in-kazakhstan/

- Early, B. R. (2009). Trading with Sanctioned States. *The University of Georgia*.
- Elhiraika, A.B., Mbate, M. (2014), Assessing the Determinants of Export Diversification in Africa, *Applied Econometrics and International Development*, 14 (1): 147-160.
- Eurasian Economic Union Export and Import Services. (n.d.). Retrieved from http://www.eurasiancommission.org/ru/act/integr_i_makroec/dep_stat/fin_stat/express_information/Pages/exppress_ex_im_services.aspx
- Eurasian Economic Union. (2018, April 18). Экспорт и импорт услуг государств – членов Евразийского экономического союза. Retrieved April 30, 2019, from http://www.eurasiancommission.org/ru/act/integr_i_makroec/dep_stat/fin_stat/express_information/Documents/services/Express_services_4Q2017.pdf
- Eurasian Economic Union. (2019, April 19). Экспорт и импорт услуг государств – членов Евразийского экономического союза. Retrieved April 30, 2019, from http://www.eurasiancommission.org/ru/act/integr_i_makroec/dep_stat/fin_stat/express_information/Documents/services/Express_services_4Q2018.pdf
- Eurasian Economic Union. (n.d.). Retrieved April 13, 2019, from http://www.eaeunion.org/?lang=en#about-info
- Eurostat. (2016). European statistics. Retrieved April 02, 2019, from https://ec.europa.eu/eurostat/data/database
- Executive Order on implementing Russian-Chinese agreement on cooperation in gas supplies from Russia to China via the 'eastern route'. (2015, August 10). Retrieved April 01, 2019, from http://en.kremlin.ru/catalog/countries/CN/events/50116
- Executive Order on measures to ensure Russia's national security and protection of Russian citizens against criminal and other illegal acts and on the application of special economic measures against Turkey (2015). In *President of Russia*. Retrieved March 21, 2019, from http://en.kremlin.ru/events/president/news/50805

- Executive Order on special economic measures to protect Russia's security (2014). In *President of Russia.* Retrieved from http://en.kremlin.ru/events/president/news/46404
- Export Diversification and Quality. (n.d.). Retrieved April 26, 2019, from http://data.imf.org/?sk=A093DF7D-E0B8-4913-80E0-A07CF90B44DB
- Eyler, R. (2007). Economic Sanctions International Policy and Political Economy at Work. *Palgrave Macmillan.*
- Ezzati, M. (2016). Analyzing Direct and Indirect Effects of Economic Sanctions on I. R. Iran Economic Growth: Focusing on the External Sector of the Economy. *Open Journal of Marine Science.*
- Field, A.P. (2009). Discovering statistics using SPSS: and sex and drugs and rock 'n' roll. *SAGE.*
- Galanina, A. (2017, June 14). Санкции без последствий. Retrieved April 24, 2019, from https://iz.ru/606180/angelina-galanina/prodlenie-sanktcii-ne-pugaet-rossiian
- GDP of Russia (2019). In *Trading Economics.* Retrieved from https://tradingeconomics.com/russia/gdp
- Gilligan, E. (2016). Smart Sanctions Against Russia: Human Rights, Magnitsky and the Ukrainian Crisis. *Demokratizatsiya: The Journal of Post-Soviet Democratization*, *24*(2).
- Gottemoeller, R. (2007). The Evolution of Sanctions in Practice and Theory. *Survival*, *49*(4), 99-110.
- Grieve, R. H. (1983). Adam Smith's 'Wealth of Nations': the Legacy of a Great Scottish Economist. *ResearchGate.*
- Haidar, J. I. (2016). Sanctions and Export Deflection: Evidence from Iran. *Economic Policy 63rd Panel Meeting.*
- Hausmann, R., Hwang, J., & Rodrik, D. (2006), What You Export Matters, *CEPR Discussion Papers 5444.*
- Haynes, J., Hough, P., Malik, S., & Pettiford, L. (2013). *World Politics: International Relations and Globalisation in the 21st Century.* N.p.: Routledge.
- Haynes, J., Hough, P., Malik, S., & Pettiford, L. (2017). *World Politics: International Relations and Globalisation in the 21st Century.* N.p.: SAGE.

- Hesse, H. (2007), Export diversification and economic growth, *The World Bank.*
- Hirschman, A. (1945). National Power and the Structure of Foreign Trade. *University of California Press.*
- Hitt, M.A., Tihanyi, L., Miller, T., & Connelly, B. (2006). International diversification: antecedents, outcomes, and moderators. *J. Manage*. 32 (6), 831–867.
- Hoskisson, R. E., & Hitt, M. A. (1990). Antecedents and Performance Outcomes of Diversification: A Review and Critique of Theoretical Perspectives. *SAGE Journal.*
- Hsieh, H., & Shannon, S. E. (2005). Three Approaches to Qualitative Content Analysis. *Qualitative Health Research, 15*(9)
- Hufbauer, G. C., Schott, J. J., Elliott, K. A., & Oegg, B. (2007). *Economic sanctions reconsidered* (3rd ed.). Washington, DC: Peterson Institute for International Economics.
- Hurriyet Daily News. (2018, April 22). Russia-Turkey investment fund 'to enhance bilateral ties' - Latest News. Retrieved April 14, 2019, from http://www.hurriyetdailynews.com/russia-turkey-investment-fund-to-enhance-bilateral-ties-130690
- Hurriyet Daily News. (2018, August 27). Europe should react to US sanctions targeting Turkey, China, Russia: German FM - World News. Retrieved April 11, 2019, from http://www.hurriyetdailynews.com/europe-should-react-to-us-sanctions-targeting-turkey-china-turkey-german-fm-136189
- Hurriyet Daily News. (2019). Russia-Turkey investment fund 'to enhance bilateral ties' - Latest News. Retrieved April 14, 2019, from http://www.hurriyetdailynews.com/russia-turkey-investment-fund-to-enhance-bilateral-ties-130690
- Joint Declaration between the Republic of Turkey and the Russian Federation on Progress towards a New Stage in Relations and Further Deepening of Friendship and Multidimentional Partnership (2009). In *Republic of Turkey Ministry of Foreign Affairs*. Retrieved from http://www.mfa.gov.tr/joint-declaration-between-the-republic-of-turkey-and-the-russian-federation-on-progress-

towards-a-new-stage-in-relations-and-further-deepening-of-friendship-and-multidimentional-

- Kaempfer, W. H., & Lowenberg, A. D. (2007). The Political Economy of Economic Sanctions. *Elsevier B.V.*, *2*, 868-910.
- Kirshner, J. (1997). The micro-foundations of economic sanctions. *Security Studies*, *6*(3), 32-64.
- Kondracki, N. L., & Wellman, N. S. (2002). Content analysis: Review of methods and their applications in nutrition education. *Journal of Nutrition Education and Behavior*, *34*, 224-230.
- Law on ratification of Russia-China cooperation agreement on developing Klyuchevskoye gold ore deposit. (2018, August 03). Retrieved April 05, 2019, from http://en.kremlin.ru/catalog/countries/CN/events/58199
- Law on ratifying agreement and protocol between Russia and China on avoiding double taxation. (2016, January 31). Retrieved April 01, 2019, from http://en.kremlin.ru/catalog/countries/CN/events/51244
- Law on ratifying agreement and protocol between Russia and China on avoiding double taxation (2016). In *President of Russia.* Retrieved from http://en.kremlin.ru/catalog/countries/CN/events/51244
- Law ratifying agreement on establishing the BRICS Contingent Reserve Arrangement. (2015, May 02). Retrieved March 28, 2019, from http://en.kremlin.ru/catalog/countries/CN/events/49393
- Law ratifying agreement on establishing the BRICS Contingent Reserve Arrangement (2015). In *President of Russia.* Retrieved from http://en.kremlin.ru/catalog/countries/CN/events/49393
- Law ratifying Russian-Chinese agreement on cooperation in gas supplies via the 'eastern' route (2015). In *President of Russia.* Retrieved from http://en.kremlin.ru/acts/news/49392
- Lederman, D., Maloney, W. (2007), Natural Resources: Neither Curse nor Destiny, *Stanford: Stanford University Press*.
- Lektzian, D., & Souva, M. (2003, November 1). The Economic Peace Between Democracies: Economic Sanctions and Domestic Institutions. *SAGE Journal*, *40*(6).

- Levada Center Yuri Levada Analytical Center. (2018, April 17). Retrieved April 27, 2019, from https://www.levada.ru/en/2018/12/07/sactions/
- Marinov, N. (2005). Do economic sanctions destabilize country leaders? American Journal of Political Science, 49(3), 564–576.
- Markedonov, S., & Ulchenko, N. (2011). Turkey and Russia: An Evolving Relationship. In *Carnegie Endowment for International Peace*. Retrieved from https://carnegieendowment.org/2011/08/19/turkey-and-russia-evolving-relationship-pub-45383
- Meeting with Prime Minister of Pakistan Nawaz Sharif (2015). In *President of Russia*. Retrieved from http://en.kremlin.ru/events/president/news/49911
- Meeting with Prime Minister of Pakistan Nawaz Sharif. (2015, July 10). Retrieved April 07, 2019, from http://en.kremlin.ru/catalog/countries/PK/events/49911
- Meyer, K.E. (2006). Global focusing from domestic conglomerates to global specialists. *J. Manage. Stud.* 43 (5), 1109–1144.
- Mikic, M., Gilbert, J. (2007). Trade Statistics in Policymaking: A Handbook of Commonly Used Trade Indices and Indicators. *United Nations Publication*.
- Miller, R. A. (1995). Domestic Structures and the Diversionary Use of Force. *American Journal of Political Science*, *39*(3).
- Ministry of Economic Development. (2017, August 18). Министерство экономического развития Российской Федерации. Retrieved March 18, 2019, from http://economy.gov.ru/minec/about/structure/depSectorEconom/2017180802
- Miyagawa, M. (1992). Do Economic Sanctions Work? *McMillan Press*.
- Moffatt, M. (2018). The Augmented Dickey-Fuller Test. In *ThoughtCo*. Retrieved from https://www.thoughtco.com/the-augmented-dickey-fuller-test-1145985
- Neuenkirch, M. and Neumeier, F. (2015). Always Affecting the Wrong People? The Impact of US Sanctions on Poverty, *University of Trier Research Papers in Economics*.

- Newlin, C., & Mankoff, J. (2016, December 16). U.S. Sanctions against Russia: What You Need to Know. Retrieved April 23, 2019, from https://www.csis.org/analysis/us-sanctions-against-russia-what-you-need-know
- Nincic, M., Wallensteen, P. (1983). Dilemmas of Economic Coercion: Sanctions in World Politics. *Praeger*,
- No: 207, 1 August 2018, Press Release Regarding the US Treasury Department's decision to sanction our country (2018). In *Republic of Turkey Ministry of Foreign Affairs*. Retrieved from http://www.mfa.gov.tr/no_-207_-abd-hazine-bakanliginin-ulkemizle-ilgili-olarak-acikladigi-yaptirim-karari-hk_en.en.mfa
- O'Brien, R., & Williams, M. (2013). *Global Political Economy*. N.p.: Red Globe Press.
- Oatley, T. (2004). *International Political Economy: Interests and Institutions in the Global Economy*. N.p.: Pearson/Longman.
- Oncel, A., & Liapina, L. (2018). The effects of Turkish-Russian political relations on bilateral trade balance: Cointegration and causal analysis. *Theoretical and Applied Economics*, *15*(1), 73-94.
- Önder, A. S., & Yilmazkuday, H. (2016). Trade partner diversification and growth: How trade links matter. *Journal of Macroeconomics*.
- Osakwe, P. N., Santos-Paulino, A. U., & Dogan, B. (2018). Trade dependene, liberalization and exports diversification in developing countries. *UNCTAD Research Paper*.
- Özbay, F. (2011). The Relatios Between Turkey and Russia in the 2000s. *Perceptions*, 16(3).
- Özdal, H, Özertem, H.S., Has, K. & Demirtepe, M.T. (2013). Türkiye-Rusya İlişkileri, Rekabetten Çok Yönlü İşbirliğine, *USAK Yayınları.*
- Pamuk, H. (2018, August 12). Turkey is a 'target of economic war', Erdogan says. Retrieved April 13, 2019, from https://uk.reuters.com/article/uk-turkey-currency-erdogan/erdogan-says-u-s-wrong-to-threaten-turkey-after-trump-doubles-tariffs-idUKKBN1KW08S?il=0
- Pamuk, H. (2018). Turkey eyes Trump protection from any sanctions for Russian defense purchase. In *Reuters*. Retrieved from https://www.reuters.com/article/us-

turkey-security-usa/turkey-eyes-trump-protection-from-any-sanctions-for-russian-defense-purchase-idUSKCN1RS1QY

- Parker, R. W. (2000). The problem with scorecards: How (and how not) to measure the cost-effectiveness of economic sanctions. Michigan Journal of International Law, 21.
- Pearson, A., & Sanders, L. (2019). Syria conflict: What do the US, Russia, Turkey and Iran want? In *DW*. Retrieved from https://www.dw.com/en/syria-conflict-what-do-the-us-russia-turkey-and-iran-want/a-41211604
- Peksen, D., & Son, B. (2015). Economic coercion and currency crises in target countries. *Journal of Peace Research*, *52*(4).
- Project (2019). In *TurkStream*. Retrieved from http://turkstream.info/
- Project History (2019). In *Akkuyu NPP*. Retrieved from http://www.akkunpp.com/project-history-2
- Prokopenko, A. (2018, December 20). Putin's Courtiers: How Sanctions Have Changed Russia's Economic Policy. Retrieved March 17, 2019, from https://carnegie.ru/commentary/78008
- Ravenhill, J. (2005). *Global Political Economy*. N.p.: Oxford University Press.
- Regions of Russia. (2017, August 18). Александр Масленников: Санкции сделали нас сильнее! Retrieved March 18, 2019, from http://www.gosrf.ru/news/31325/
- Revealed Comparative Advantage (2019). In *UNCTAD Stat*. Retrieved from https://unctadstat.unctad.org/EN/RcaRadar.html
- Rosoboron Export. (n.d.). Partner countries and joint projects. Retrieved March 30, 2019, from http://roe.ru/eng/rosoboronexport/partner-countries/
- Russia and China have signed a major gas supply contract (2014). In *President of Russia*. Retrieved from http://en.kremlin.ru/events/president/news/21063
- Russia and Turkey have established the High-Level Cooperation Council (2010). In *President of Russia*. Retrieved from http://en.kremlin.ru/events/president/news/7723
- Russia Economic Report (2018). In *The World Bank*. Retrieved from http://www.worldbank.org/en/country/russia/publication/rer

- Russia GDP Growth Rate (2019). In *The World Bank*. Retrieved from https://data.worldbank.org/indicator/NY.GDP.MKTP.KD.ZG?locations=RU
- Russia Inflation Rate (2019). In *Trading Economics*. Retrieved from https://tradingeconomics.com/russia/inflation-cpi
- Russia reacts over US sanctions against Turkey (2018). In *World Bulletin*. Retrieved from https://www.worldbulletin.net/europe/russia-reacts-over-us-sanctions-against-turkey-h204618.html
- Russia's Lavrov, in Turkey, calls U.S. sanctions policy illegitimate (2018). In *Reuters*. Retrieved from https://www.reuters.com/article/russia-turkey-us-sanctions/russias-lavrov-in-turkey-calls-u-s-sanctions-policy-illegitimate-idUSR4N1V0039
- Russian Direct Investment Fund. (n.d.). Partnerships. Retrieved February 19, 2019, from https://rdif.ru/Eng_Partnership/
- Sanctions Against Russia (2019). In *EU Sanctions Map*. Retrieved March 14, 2019, from https://www.sanctionsmap.eu/#/main/details/26/?search=%7B%22value%22:%22%22,%22searchType%22:%7B%7D%7D
- Sanctions List Serch (2019). In *Office of Foreign Assets Control*. Retrieved March 8, 2019, from https://sanctionssearch.ofac.treas.gov/
- Shanghai Cooperation Organisation (2019). In *Republic of Turkey Ministry of Foreign Affairs*. Retrieved from http://www.mfa.gov.tr/shanghai-cooperation-organization.en.mfa
- Speech at a ceremony marking the 15th anniversary of signing of the Treaty on Good-Neighbourliness, Friendship and Cooperation between the Russian Federation and the People's Republic of China. (2016, June 25). Retrieved April 01, 2019, from http://en.kremlin.ru/catalog/countries/CN/events/52274
- Spence, M., Jones, D. (2007), Wealth of Nations: How Poor Countries Get Richer.
- Sputnik. (2018, August 16). ABD'nin Türkiye'ye yönelik yaptırımları. Retrieved February 27, 2019, from https://tr.sputniknews.com/infografik/201808151034772132-abd-turkiye-yaptirim-dolar-euro-tl-doviz/

- Strange, S. (1970). International Economics and International Relations: A Case of Mutual Neglect. *International Affairs (Royal Institute of International Affairs 1944-)*, *46*(2).
- Sudagezer, E. (2018, September 05). Türk halkının yüzde 74'ü dolara karşı yerel para birimiyle ticareti savunuyor, ABD'yle ittifaka destek yalnızca yüzde 4.4. Retrieved April 28, 2019, from https://tr.sputniknews.com/turkiye/201809051035064500-turkiye-yerel-para-birimiyle-ticaret-dolar-abd-ittifak-optimar-arastirma/
- Süsler, B. (2018). EU and Turkey on same side against US. In *EU Observer*. Retrieved from https://euobserver.com/opinion/142647
- The concept of economic diversification in the context of response measures. Technical paper by the secretariat (2007). In *UNFCCC*. Retrieved from https://unfccc.int/sites/default/files/resource/Technical%20paper_Economic%20diversification.pdf
- The Observatory of Economic Complexity. (n.d.). Retrieved April 15, 2019, from https://atlas.media.mit.edu/en/profile/country/tur/#Destinations
- The World Bank. (n.d.). Trade Indicators. Retrieved April 10, 2019, from https://wits.worldbank.org/wits/wits/witshelp/Content/Utilities/e1.trade_indicators.htm
- Torbakov, I. (2008). The Georgia Crisis and Russia-Turkey Relations. *The Jamestown Foundation*.
- Trade Database (2019). In *UN COMTRADE*. Retrieved from https://comtrade.un.org/data/
- Treasury Sanctions Turkish Officials with Leading Roles in Unjust Detention of U.S. Pastor Andrew Brunson (2018). In *US Department of Treasury Press Releases*. Retrieved from https://home.treasury.gov/news/press-releases/sm453
- Troianovski, A. (2018). Russia keeps getting hit with sanctions. Do they make a difference? In *Msn News*. Retrieved from https://www.msn.com/en-ie/news/world/russia-keeps-getting-hit-with-sanctions-do-they-make-a-difference/ar-BBMjTlV?li=AA54um
- Turkey Exports to and Imports from Russia (2017). In *WITS*. Retrieved from https://wits.worldbank.org/countrystats.aspx?lang=en

- Turkey Foreign Direct Investment (2019). In *Trading Economics*. Retrieved from https://tradingeconomics.com/turkey/foreign-direct-investment
- Turkey Letter to UNSC on Shooting Down SU-24 Plane. (2015, November 24). Retrieved March 18, 2019, from https://tr.scribd.com/doc/291002800/Turkey-Letter-to-UNSC-on-Shooting-Down-SU-24-Plane-Nov-24-2015
- Turkey never supported anti-Russian sanctions — top diplomat (2018). In *TASS Russian News Agency*. Retrieved from http://tass.com/world/1017180
- TÜRSAB. (2019). Turizm Gelirleri (Tourism Revenue). Retrieved April 04, 2019, from https://www.tursab.org.tr/istatistikler-icerik/turizm-geliri
- Unemployment Rate (2019). In *The World Bank- The Global Economy*. Retrieved from https://www.theglobaleconomy.com/Russia/Unemployment_rate/
- Veseth, M. (2007). What is International Political Economy?
- Yang, J., Askari, H., Teegen, H. (2004). U.S. Economic Sanctions: An Empirical Study. *The International Trade Journal* 28(1).

Appendix

Below you can find the all of the logarithmic regressions including the main one, total trade between Russia and Turkey, and other additional three regressions of selected traded products (Fuels, Metals and Vegetables).

Model 1 (All):

$$\text{Ln}\ (\text{Trade}_{\text{All}}) = \alpha + \beta_1\ \text{GDP}_{\text{TR}} + \beta_2\ \text{GDP}_{\text{RUS}} + \beta_3\ \ln\ \text{FDI}_{\text{TR}} + \beta_4\ \ln\ \text{FDI}_{\text{RUS}} + \beta_5\ \text{SANC}_{\text{TR}} + \beta_6\ \text{SANC}_{\text{RUS}} + \beta_7\ \ln\ \text{Trade}_{t-1} + \varepsilon_{\text{All}}$$

Model 2 (Fuels):

$$\text{Ln}\ (\text{Trade}_{\text{Fuels}}) = \alpha + \beta_1\ \text{GDP}_{\text{TR}} + \beta_2\ \text{GDP}_{\text{RUS}} + \beta_3\ \ln\ \text{FDI}_{\text{TR}} + \beta_4\ \ln\ \text{FDI}_{\text{RUS}} + \beta_5\ \text{SANC}_{\text{TR}} + \beta_6\ \text{SANC}_{\text{RUS}} + \beta_7\ \ln\ \text{Trade}_{t-1} + \varepsilon_{\text{All}}$$

Model 3 (Metals):

$$\text{Ln}\ (\text{Trade}_{\text{Metals}}) = \alpha + \beta_1\ \text{GDP}_{\text{TR}} + \beta_2\ \text{GDP}_{\text{RUS}} + \beta_3\ \ln\ \text{FDI}_{\text{TR}} + \beta_4\ \ln\ \text{FDI}_{\text{RUS}} + \beta_5\ \text{SANC}_{\text{TR}} + \beta_6\ \text{SANC}_{\text{RUS}} + \beta_7\ \ln\ \text{Trade}_{t-1} + \varepsilon_{\text{All}}$$

Model 4 (Vegetables):

$$\text{Ln}\ (\text{Trade}_{\text{Vegetables}}) = \alpha + \beta_1\ \text{GDP}_{\text{TR}} + \beta_2\ \text{GDP}_{\text{RUS}} + \beta_3\ \ln\ \text{FDI}_{\text{TR}} + \beta_4\ \ln\ \text{FDI}_{\text{RUS}} + \beta_5\ \text{SANC}_{\text{TR}} + \beta_6\ \text{SANC}_{\text{RUS}} + \beta_7\ \ln\ \text{Trade}_{t-1} + \varepsilon_{\text{All}}$$